KPI Checklists

Develop meaningful, trusted, KPIs and
reports using step-by-step checklists

Bernie Smith

Metric Press
Sheffield, England

Published by Metric Press
60 Bromwich Road
Sheffield S8 0GG
Tel.: +44(0)208 133 9440
Email: bernie.smith@madetomeasureKPIs.co.uk
Website: http://www.madetomeasureKPIs.com

First published in Great Britain in 2013

ISBN: 978-1-910047-00-2

British Library Cataloguing-in-Publication Data
A catalogue record for this book is available from the British Library

Library of Congress Cataloguing-in-Publication Data
A catalogue record for this book is available from the Library of Congress

Printed and bound in Great Britain

KPI Checklists

Contents

Acknowledgements

I have attempted a number of things in life where I have seriously underestimated the time, effort and commitment needed to complete them. Of these efforts, none has been tougher to complete than writing this book (with the exception of helping raise two children and I'm still working on that). Without lots of patient help I would never have finished it. I am particularly grateful to Liz, Jenny, David Bishop, Kate Stott and Richard Holloway. I am also grateful to all those who sounded genuinely interested when I told them about this project.

Introduction

Who this book is for

This book is for people who:

- Have the task of creating new KPIs for their organisation.
- Have been asked to improve or enhance existing KPIs.
- Need help with the practicalities of implementing a measurement system.

If you follow the steps laid out in this book you should end up with a measurement system that meets your needs. Crucially, you will have a structured and documented record showing how and why the system was developed in that way. You will also be clear on the limitations and assumptions that were made along the way - invaluable for future improvement.

About the author

Bernie Smith coaches businesses to develop meaningful KPIs and present their management information in the clearest possible way to support good decision making.

As owner of Made to Measure KPIs he has worked with major organisations including UBS, Lloyd's Register, Scottish Widows, Tesco Bank, Yorkshire Building Society, RSA and many others.

Previously, Bernie led teams delivering operational improvement in FTSE 100 companies using Lean and Six Sigma approaches. This took him to the US to help paper makers, Finland, to make olefins and Wrexham to package cheese.

Bernie lives in Sheffield, UK, with his wife and two children and some underused exercise equipment.

Why this book was written

One of the things that has become very clear, no matter what the industry, is that businesses that don't have a clear idea of what they're trying to improve invariably get disappointing results.

It may seem that KPIs are something that you should just be able to pick up off-the-shelf and use, like a piece of software or a template. The truth is that KPIs are a detailed representation of **your** specific business and of **your** aspirations for **your** business.

KPI books normally fall into one of three camps:

- They talk about lofty organisational goals and strategy.
- They're interested in software and the mechanics of measurement.
- They focus in on a very particular type of management e.g. HR or sales performance.

This book does not fit into any of these categories. It is intended to be a practical step-by-step guide that will take you from early questions around 'What is it you are trying to achieve in this business?' through 'How do you cascade this to the right people and make sure you drive the right behaviour?' to 'How do you physically collect this information and make sure it gets analysed in as pain-free a way as possible?'

I realise this is the kind of book you will be reading because you have an objective to achieve, not for entertainment, so it is designed so you can jump between sections depending on your need - just make sure you don't skip the critical steps though.

Guide to icons

Key Idea

Crucial concepts are flagged with a key idea icon. It is well worth reading these before using the checklists as they help lay the conceptual foundations.

True Story

Although this book is very checklist centric, I have added a few experiences and stories along the way. They bring some of the advice to life and offer some relief from the lists.

Example

Examples are used to explain how principles and techniques are applied.

Trap

There are some traps for the unwary. This icon flags up some of the ones I have witnessed or fallen into myself.

Tip

Sometimes there are short cuts or better ways of doing things. Look for this big thumb for practical tips.

Checklist

The main attraction of this book is checklists. There are lots of them and they are clearly marked with this icon.

You can download any templates I mention from my website. Here's the shortlink: **http://wp.me/p1H6XP-zD**

Key Idea

What is a KPI?

First of all, let's be clear what we mean by a KPI. The literal meaning is 'key performance indicator'.

Just knowing what the initials stand for is not that helpful. So what does it really mean?

- **Key** means it... 'provides a means of achieving or understanding something'.
- **Performance** means... 'a particular action, deed, or proceeding'.
- **Indicator** means... 'a thing that indicates the state or level of something'.

Put in simpler language, a KPI is a thing that:

- shows you how you are doing at...
- a particular activity...
- to achieve a particular level or outcome.

In fact, it's pretty much exactly the same thing as a 'measure' or 'metric'. The only real difference is the word 'key' implies that it is 'really important'. I will generally use KPI in this book. Take KPI, metric and measure as interchangeable.

Why Finance should not own (all) your KPIs

One important point to make is that KPIs are not just financial measures. Financial measures are crucial in many organisations, but they are also 'lagging' - which means they tell you what happened after the event. KPIs should also help you see what is coming, not just what has passed. It's like the difference between a rear view mirror (lagging indicator) and having a windscreen (leading indicator). You need both. Life becomes considerably riskier without a clear view of the road ahead. A good dashboard or balanced scorecard will have a mixture of financial and non-financial, leading and lagging indicators.

Key Idea

The seven steps to KPI bliss

The approach of this book is to follow a series of structured steps known as the Results Orientated KPI System or ROKS.

These steps start with making sure your strategic objectives are crystal clear and take you all the way to a fully functional dashboard or report. There are seven main steps, each broken down into sub-steps. This means there are a lot of stages in the method but this is to make it as easy as possible to follow. Each step consists of:

- A short description.
- An example, illustration or story to help understanding.
- A series of checklists showing key steps, questions or requirements to help you get through that step successfully.

The main steps are shown in Fig. 0.1. Don't worry too much about trying to figure out the subtleties of each, that's what the rest of the book is about...

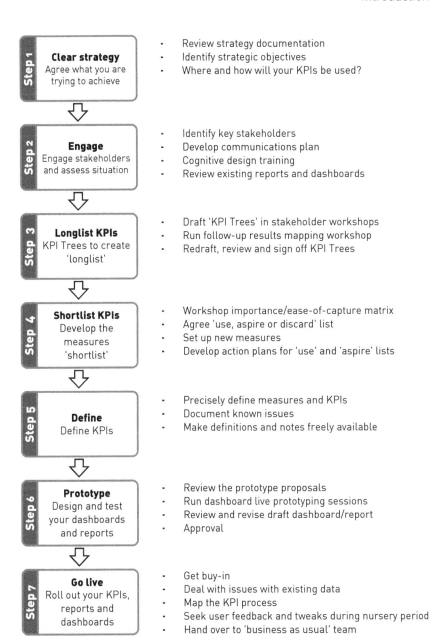

Step 1
Clear strategy
Agree what you are trying to achieve
- Review strategy documentation
- Identify strategic objectives
- Where and how will your KPIs be used?

Step 2
Engage
Engage stakeholders and assess situation
- Identify key stakeholders
- Develop communications plan
- Cognitive design training
- Review existing reports and dashboards

Step 3
Longlist KPIs
KPI Trees to create 'longlist'
- Draft 'KPI Trees' in stakeholder workshops
- Run follow-up results mapping workshop
- Redraft, review and sign off KPI Trees

Step 4
Shortlist KPIs
Develop the measures 'shortlist'
- Workshop importance/ease-of-capture matrix
- Agree 'use, aspire or discard' list
- Set up new measures
- Develop action plans for 'use' and 'aspire' lists

Step 5
Define
Define KPIs
- Precisely define measures and KPIs
- Document known issues
- Make definitions and notes freely available

Step 6
Prototype
Design and test your dashboards and reports
- Review the prototype proposals
- Run dashboard live prototyping sessions
- Review and revise draft dashboard/report
- Approval

Step 7
Go live
Roll out your KPIs, reports and dashboards
- Get buy-in
- Deal with issues with existing data
- Map the KPI process
- Seek user feedback and tweaks during nursery period
- Hand over to 'business as usual' team

Fig. 0.1: The 'Results Orientated KPI System' process steps

Why use checklists?

I'm a huge fan of checklists. If you have used them and love them, great. If you need some persuasion then I'd strongly recommend 'The Checklist Manifesto' by Atul Gawande. It's a very readable and highly compelling explanation of how checklists can help just about any enterprise, how they work and when to use them. Full details of his book are in the Bibliography.

One of the things I learnt from Gawande's book was that checklists can be traced back to a US Air Force competition in 1935.

True Story

The history of checklists - Inspiration from the ashes

In the summer of 1934 the US Air Corps proposed replacing the B-10 bomber with a new multi-engined bomber. It had to be able to fly at least 1,020 miles, be able to carry a 2,000 pound bomb load and reach at least 200 mph. The specification was circulated to the major aircraft manufacturers. Their prototypes would be evaluated in a competition.

Realising that they could not substantially improve on the existing designs for twin engined planes, Boeing went for a radical, four-engined design. Working in complete secrecy, Boeing devised the Model 299.

It took its maiden flight in July 1935 and had innovations such as wing flaps for better performance at low speeds, electric trim tabs on its control surfaces for improved handling, hydraulically operated constant-speed propeller and a host of other new ideas.

It created a sensation and was quickly dubbed the 'Flying Fortress' in the press. It was the clear favourite to win the competition, exceeding all the specification requirements by a massive margin. There was nobody to meet it as it was flown in for delivery to the assessment in Dayton. 'No one expected it for another hour', such was its speed.

On October 30th 1935 the prototype took off, watched by a crowd of spectators. Leslie R. Tower, Boeing's senior test pilot, was observing. At the controls was Major Ployer P. Hill, the Air Corps' chief test pilot. The plane rose to 300 feet, stalled, rolled to the side and crashed back into the airfield, exploding.

Investigation showed a recently added safety feature, a lock on the elevator, had not been turned off before take-off. The lock was intended to stop the control surfaces being damaged by high winds when the plane was on the ground.

The mechanism was controlled from the cockpit, but no one remembered to turn it off before take-off, causing the stall. This was despite the involvement of Tower - who probably knew more about the plane than anyone alive - and Hill, the Air Corps' top test pilot.

The General Staff concluded that 'Because the airplane crashed, it must be too complex for anyone to handle safely.' They went on to order 133 competitor aircraft, the Douglas B-18 Bolo.

It was a devastating blow for Boeing, almost putting them out of business.

Still convinced of the benefits of the Flying Fortress, a group of test pilots decided to use a novel approach. Rather than focusing on 'more training', they came up with a simple list of things that should be checked before and during take-off.

Armed with this new approach, and using a legal loophole that enabled the Air Corps to buy a further 13 aircraft for 'testing', they were able to fly 1.8 million miles in the Model 299 without incident. The US Air Corps were slowly won round to the merits of the model, eventually ordering nearly 13,000 of them.

The legacy of this outside of aviation was the very simple but powerful concept of the checklist. It enables humans, with our unreliable memories, to handle high levels of complexity with confidence and ease.

Measurement and reporting has become increasingly complex. Checklists are the ideal tool to help both with implementation and everyday running of those processes.

Agree what you are trying to achieve

Is your strategy fit for purpose?

Imagine a friend asking 'Can you pop out to the hardware store and buy a tool for me?' Obviously your first question would be 'What kind of tool are you looking for?'

Deciding on your measures and KPIs without having a clear business strategy is like going tool shopping without knowing what it is that you are trying to achieve or what tool you need.

Trap

Be wary of 'off-the-shelf' KPI sets

It's also equally risky to use so-called 'off-the-shelf' KPIs if you don't make any attempt to customise or filter the selection you are offered. Imagine being told by a complete stranger 'The hammer is the most useful tool a manager can buy.' If your issue is nail-related then she may have a point. If you have a wood-size issue then you may have a pretty compelling argument that the saw is the king of the tool kit. Without a clear picture of what you are trying to achieve, any debates about the relative merits of 'this KPI over that one' becomes completely unstructured and pointless.

Being clear on what you are trying to achieve through measurement is 100% essential and unavoidable. If you skip this crucial step you only achieve your organisational objectives by accident.

The next step, after nailing down your strategy, is to break this down into a little bit more detail. This next level we call strategic objectives, or long-term organisational goals.

Sticking with the DIY theme, I particularly like the vision statement of B&Q (a very large UK DIY chain):

'We have a vision at B&Q: to be the first place anyone thinks of when they think of home improvement, and the only place they need to go.'

I like this as it is very clear how it can be broken down into specific and measurable outcomes:

- **To be the first place anyone thinks of when they think of home improvement** - This can be directly measured through market research showing customer recall of DIY brands. We can also look at relative footfall, repeat visits etc. to build a more nuanced view.

- **The only place they need to go** - There are some very clear and measurable specifics around product lines, customer needs and stock management.

I'm sure this mission statement could be improved but it certainly beats the usual bland and generic mission statements focused on 'service' and 'realising people are our most valuable asset'. It's probably worth adding that B&Q would have other strategic objectives that are not customer-related but these two certainly make a good starting point.

Example

Example

If my personal strategy is to 'Be the first external support that a UK FTSE 100 financial services senior manager contacts when they need KPI and measurement help', then my strategic objectives might be:

- Become the most sought after UK author on KPIs and measurement.
- Develop a visible and frequently visited online and social media presence - outperforming alternative UK-based offers.
- Deliver more than six months of KPI-related projects to FTSE 100 UK financial services firms each year.

Even though I've not put many specific measurable targets in there, they are quite specific without being too narrow. Watch out for woolly objectives, with words like 'excellence', 'aspire', 'fantastic', 'best in breed' and 'great', as you will end up having endless debate about what 'brilliant' actually means. I was involved in just that debate for at least an hour, with a group of very bright and motivated individuals. We still could not agree at the end of the debate.

It is far better to start with a bit of clarity. If you are saddled with poorly worded strategic objectives then you have some work to do to make them clearer and more specific.

A good indicator that you are at the right level of detail is the number of strategic objectives. You should expect to have between two and seven. Fewer than three and you are probably not breaking your strategy down enough, more than seven and you risk confusing people and having a fragmented approach.

Tip

This book isn't intended to help you develop your strategy. There are lots of excellent books to help you do this. I would particularly recommend the Harvard Business Review's book 'On Strategy' which comprises 10 definitive and surprisingly readable articles on strategy (full details at the back of this book).

What is crucial is that your strategy is fit for the job intended.

Now hopefully your organisation has a clear strategy, broken down into objectives in a readily accessible form. If it has, then you need to get hold of it and read it a few times. Once you have done that, use the checklist I have included on the next page to show whether it's going to do the job for you:

Checklist

Strategy fitness

❏   Is the strategy written down?

❏   Does the strategy make sense to an intelligent, but non-specialist, reader?

❏   Is there broad management consensus that the strategy is correct?

❏ Is your strategy relevant to the key decision-makers in the business? (Do any of them dismiss it when you discuss it with them?)

❏ Is your strategy linked to clear and specific **strategic objectives**?

❏ Are the strategic objective descriptions physically accessible by all the managers within the organisation? Do they have easy access to a paper or electronic copy?

❏ Are the strategic objectives broad and 'non-dated' (rather than simply being important actions that will be completed at some point)?

❏ Are managers across the organisation familiar with the strategic objectives, without scrambling onto the intranet or looking for bits of paper?

❏ Are the key decision-makers either working to the strategy or attempting to work to the strategy?

❏ Is the current strategy still relevant to the business situation and up to date?

❏ Are there fewer than seven strategic objectives?

If the answer to each of the questions above is 'yes', then you are in a great position to start developing your measures. If one or more of your answers is 'no', then much of your hard work could be undone if you start to create measures without fixing the problems with your strategy.

The very first workshop I ran after setting up Made to Measure KPIs, to create measures for a large not-for-profit organisation, rapidly identified that there was no clear strategy for that organisation. Instead of developing a working set of measures, as planned, we ended up spending a large chunk of the session debating what our strategic objectives should be. I learned early on that no strategy equals no meaningful measures.

A clear strategy that creates an aligned set of measures will mean that most people in the organisation are pushing in the same direction at the same time. A badly designed set of measures and KPIs will mean that alignment and collaboration are likely to be random and poorly controlled.

True Story

Perfect chaos

Just to underline this point, here's a story about when I worked with a financial services firm that felt the error rate in their process was strategically important. They created a scorecard that focused almost entirely on the 'right first time' rate and linked it directly with their staff's personal bonuses. If they hit 99.9% quality they would get their bonus. Funnily enough, almost everyone got their accuracy bonus but the volume of complaints trebled in the two years after the measure/reward scheme was introduced.

What is the difference between a strategic objective and a mission statement?

There is a bit of a blurry line between mission statements and strategic objectives. Often clues to the strategic objectives are contained within a mission statement. Here are some notable vision/mission statements from history.

Example

A grim mission statement

General Motors: 'GM is a multinational corporation engaged in socially responsible operations, worldwide. It is dedicated to provide products and services of such quality that our customers will receive superior value while our employees and business partners will share our success and our stockholders will receive a sustained superior return on their investment.'

Three good mission statements

Innocent: 'Make natural, delicious food and drink that helps people live well and die old'.

National Multiple Sclerosis Society: 'A World Free of MS.'

Microsoft: 'A computer on every desk and in every home.'

I like these because they are short, clearly carefully-considered, distinctive and you can see how a set of unique, and measurable, KPIs could spring up to support the statement.

A funny mission statement

Newport News Shipbuilding and Drydock Company Mission Statement: 'We will build great ships. At a profit if we can. At a loss if we must. But we will build great ships.'

Checklist

Are your strategic objectives clear?

❏ Is each strategic objective articulated in no more than two sentences?

❏ Does the description of the strategic objective make sense?

❏ Is it possible to interpret a statement in a radically different way? (Best test this by getting a number of different people to read and explain back what a given statement means - there can be very surprising variations.)

❏ Are there any 'woolly words' or 'management buzzwords' in the strategic objective? Examples of words that don't help include 'synergy', 'excellence', 'outstanding' and 'empowerment' - they sound great but are very hard to pin down. If there are, then these need to be removed or replaced with clear, simple phrases.

If your strategy is not available in this form then you will need to have a session with the leaders in your organisation to make sure that you can distil the strategy into something suitable.

Here are some examples of clear strategic objectives:

- Increase bank capital ratio to 11%.
- Reduce loss of life through road accidents by 50%.
- Become the biggest UK supplier of rubber ducks.
- Be the fastest-delivering mail order memory stick retailer.
- Have the widest selection of digital delivery channels in Europe.

You need your strategic objectives in this very specific form to support the next steps in the ROKS process.

Engage stakeholders and assess your situation

The challenge of managing change and complexity

Because organisations are complex structures and the people within them are often anxious and busy, the 'Engagement' step is one of the easiest steps to mess up. Just working out who to talk to can be a serious challenge.

Here are some key things you need to tackle during this step:

- **Who to talk to** - You need to identify all those who have involvement in your new measures, whether in production, review or reward.
- **How deeply to engage with them** - Not all stakeholders need the same level of engagement. You need a method to manage this.
- **What the 'message' is** - KPIs can scare people. Sometimes this is a rational response, sometimes not. Simply ignoring the issues is a recipe for disaster so you need a clear understanding of what message you are trying to convey to stakeholders.
- **How you communicate** - A communications plan is needed for all but the simplest implementations. This should cover method, timing, audience, message and outcomes.
- **Stakeholder receptiveness** - Introducing new concepts, such as a radically different dashboard design, can upset stakeholders, even if they are excellent and innovative. Substantial changes should be backed up by good-quality discussion and training. The sessions should cover both the reasoning and science behind the changes.

Why develop a communications plan?

Using a communications plan does two things. Firstly, it makes sure you carefully consider what you say, to whom and when - pretty obvious. The second, slightly less obvious, point is that it provides tangible evidence it has been done properly. There will always be complaints about poor communication but the best way to show that your communications plan was properly implemented is to:

- Discuss and share the plan in advance.
- Document progress against the communications plan during the implementation.
- Evidence the delivery through a completed plan, after the event.

Build a communications plan

The sophistication of the communications plan will depend on a number of factors. Political sensitivity, number of people affected, degree of change and complexity of the implementation will all play a part. Use the following checklist to create your communications plan:

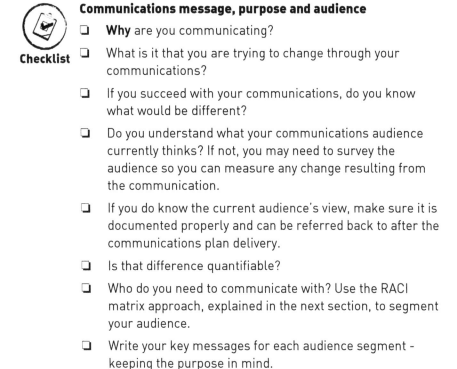

Checklist

Communications message, purpose and audience

❏ **Why** are you communicating?

❏ What is it that you are trying to change through your communications?

❏ If you succeed with your communications, do you know what would be different?

❏ Do you understand what your communications audience currently thinks? If not, you may need to survey the audience so you can measure any change resulting from the communication.

❏ If you do know the current audience's view, make sure it is documented properly and can be referred back to after the communications plan delivery.

❏ Is that difference quantifiable?

❏ Who do you need to communicate with? Use the RACI matrix approach, explained in the next section, to segment your audience.

❏ Write your key messages for each audience segment - keeping the purpose in mind.

Checklist

Designing communications activities

❏ **Delivery method** - Will it be face-to-face, by email, intranet or teleconference?

❏ **Timing** - When will you communicate? How many updates or reminders will they receive?

❏ **Owner** - Who will deliver the communications? Will they be trained? Are they suitable and motivated?

❏ **Audience** - Are you completely clear about who is included in the communications and what type of communications they will receive?

❏ **Target outcomes from communications** - What do you want the audience to know, think or do as a result of the communications?

Checklist

Deliver your communications

❏ Who will deliver the message?

❏ What preparation do they need?

❏ Have you drafted 'frequently asked questions and responses' and other backup resources for your deliverers?

❏ How many people will you need to ensure you cover all the target audience?

❏ What other resources do you need? E.g. company intranet pages, dedicated SharePoint sites etc.

❏ How can your audience feed back comments and questions?

❏ What checks do you have in place to make sure the plan is delivered as intended?

❏ How can you tell if the communication has been effective?

❏ How will you know if further communication, over and above the plan, is needed?

Checklist

Get the message and delivery right

The depth and method of delivery will be determined by:

- The time available.
- The number of people to be engaged.
- The geographical distribution of those people.
- The communications resource available - especially people to present road shows etc.
- The level of controversy/complexity in the message.
- The ability/existing knowledge of the audience.

Key communications principles

Checklist

❏ Use targeting to make sure you don't encourage people to ignore your communications.

❏ Put yourself 'in the shoes' of your audience. Look at things from their perspective and try to provide them with what they need to know.

❏ Senior endorsement can help make sure people take the message seriously, even better if the keynote communications are delivered by a senior executive.

❏ Be as honest as you can be.

❏ If you expect a bumpy ride, try and have one-to-ones with key players in advance of any group sessions to prevent the sessions becoming 'gladiatorial'.

❏ Accept that you will not always have the right information to hand. If you don't, commit to getting an answer and do so in the promised time scale.

❏ Be very, very familiar with the message.

Key Idea

Identify stakeholder types and groups

Knowing who you need to talk to, gain agreement with or keep updated is central to implementing successful measures. Many management information projects fail because of political or communications problems. This makes it especially important that you clearly identify, document and manage your stakeholders. The first step is to identify who your stakeholders are.

Stakeholders fall into these broad camps:

Data originators - The people at, or very close to, the point at which the data is collected or generated. This might be an agent or team manager in a call centre, for example.

Data aggregators - People involved in pulling the data together, but probably not analysing it. Sometimes they will be the 'data packagers' as well. Often these people are part of the company IT function.

Data packagers - The 'packagers' will perform analyses, create reports and dashboards. These people often work in a management information, business intelligence or reporting team.

Internal customers - The people who use the output from the packagers to make decisions that affect the business.

Group stakeholders based on relationship

Stakeholders are people who are involved in some way with what it is you're trying to do. To identify the key stakeholders I use a simple (and commonly used) tool called a RACI assignment matrix. It can really help clarify how you need to engage and inform your wider audience and also gives you a document for review and approval.

27

Key Idea

RACI Definitions

The initials RACI stand for:

Responsible - These are the people who do the work to achieve the task objective.

Accountable - This is the person who is ultimately answerable for correct completion of the task. This person will sign it off.

Consulted - These are people whose opinions are sought. They are often subject matter experts. It is a two-way dialogue.

Informed - People who need to be kept up to date on progress. This is not normally a two-way conversation.

The idea is to create a simple matrix. Along the top you have column headings corresponding to roles within the business - the 'Name' columns. Down the side you have either a specific KPI or report or a strategic objective or business outcome.

It will depend on the precise nature of your project and the number of measures/reports involved. On a big project it just is not practical to go down to individual measures so you need to group things in a logical way at a higher level.

You then go down the list systematically and ask yourself the question 'Is this person responsible for, accountable for, consulted about or informed about this particular KPI/objective/business outcome?'

Perspective	Objective	CEO	CFO	COO	HR Dir.
Group	Ensuring sustainability of the group and fulfilment of our mission	A	R	R	R
Financial	Increase revenue in new markets		A	R	
	Increase productivity and margin		A	R	
	Increase revenue in existing markets		A	R	
	Increase value of branding in new and existing markets	R	I	R	R
Stakeholder	Market leading services and products	I		R	
	Consistently deliver hassle-free service	I	R	R	
	Consistently deliver superior value to customers	I		A	R
Process	Improve how we understand what our customers need from us	C		C	
	Introduce innovative and high-performance services and products	I		C	
	Provide information to make sound decisions	I	C	C	
	Improve quality, cost and delivery of operating processes		R	R	R
	Deliver value from investments	I	R	R	
	Retain, develop and recruit the right people			R	A
	Deploy resources effectively			A	R
	Ensure our people are safe	A		R	R

Fig. 2.1: A sample RACI matrix

Trap

One of my clients pointed out RACI isn't in hierarchical order. In fact it should be ARCI, but this is probably best avoided!

So, to summarise, the RACI matrix gives you a neat way of grouping stakeholders by the method with which you will interact with them. It can be really useful for creating communication plans since you can refer to a complete block of stakeholders as, for example, 'informed' and reference it back to your RACI matrix.

You can further refine the matrix by grouping the names into data originators, data aggregators etc.

You can download a template from my website using this shortlink: **http://wp.me/p1H6XP-zD**

The next step is to make contact with those stakeholders.

Checklist

Talk to key stakeholders and subject matter experts

It is usually best to have a mixture of semi-structured interviews and stakeholder workshops. A semi-structured interview is one where you ask open questions and then listen carefully to the answers. When I conduct an interview I include:

Introductions

❏ About you (the interviewer), who you are and why you are here.

❏ What your objectives are, what you are looking to get from the interview.

❏ Whether the outputs are anonymous or not.

About the interviewee

❏ Their background.

❏ How long they have been in their current role.

❏   What they are looking to get from the interview.

❏   Any concerns they may have.

❏   Any questions they may have.

Open questions I ask include:

❏   Which reports, measures and dashboards are they regularly exposed to?

❏   What are their biggest worries about current reporting/ dashboarding?

❏   What single thing do they think should be the priority to improve as regards measures and reports?

❏   How confident are they in the quality of the data in their organisation?

❏   What outputs would they like to see that are not currently produced?

..And some closed questions

❏   Have the company's strategic objectives been communicated to them?

❏   Can they recall those objectives?

❏   Do they have any specific examples of measurement issues or things that need fixing urgently?

Take notes and make sure you summarise issues as you go so you can easily review your notes and develop a balanced overview.

These questions can be a bit aggressive if delivered poorly, so make sure you tread lightly in the interview and let things develop.

Stakeholder workshops

Stakeholder workshops are particularly useful when you are interested in gathering **problem-related** information or need to understand processes. Workshops are less suited to exploring more sensitive topics.

Most of the steps are the same as for a semi-structured interview, although it is wise to dwell a bit less on the background of the participants as this can make some of the more anxious group members uncomfortable.

Key points for running a successful stakeholder workshop are:

- Be clear about the purpose of the session.
- Make sure the sessions are not too big (10-12 attendees is the upper limit for one person to facilitate well).
- Be aware of management structures and make sure you don't end up with an outspoken manager and his/her tongue-tied subordinates.
- Be clear and honest about confidentiality and re-use of comments and quotes.
- Note down key points and play them back to the group at the end to make sure you have understood correctly.

Train stakeholders in quantitative visual presentation techniques

To build a consensus on how to improve management information and reporting in your organisation, it is very helpful to have some good solid theoretical underpinnings on how to communicate information clearly. If you do not have this then any design decisions can become a battle, determined by strength of will and aesthetic opinion.

There are a number of academic giants in this field, such as Edward Tufte and Stephen Few. They have written some brilliant books. Whilst the books are very interesting, they are not really in a 'how-to' format. To tackle this gap, I wrote 'BlinkReporting' which is a step-by-step guide explaining the science behind good report design and instructions on how to build a dashboard using this approach in Excel. 'BlinkReporting' is available as a download from this link or QR code:

http://www.madetomeasurekpis. com/downloads/blinkreporting-step- by-step-guide-to-creating-brilliant- reports/

Use the code **KPIChecklists50percent** for a 50% discount.

I recommend reading BlinkReporting as it explains the ideas behind the approach. If you don't have time to read it, there is a very high-level summary in **Step 6 - Prototype: Design and test your dashboards and reports** on page 71.

Tip

How to tell what people really think of a design

If your objective is to fundamentally overhaul the reports or dashboards that are produced in your organisation, it really helps to start showing people some examples from previous projects or other organisations. Often their initial reaction will tell you a great deal about what they really think of the current documents being produced. Listen very carefully to what they say they like and don't like about the samples you show them, as this can help you avoid going down blind alleys later in the process.

Here is a pair of before-and-after examples that you can use:

Daily Flash Card

	Avg of last month	Day											
		08/11/13	09/11/13	10/11/13	11/11/13	12/11/13	13/11/13	14/11/13	15/11/13	16/11/13	17/11/13	18/11/13	19/11/13
Branches													
Withdrawals Volume (£million)	19.6	15.9			31.7	17.6	15.6	17.9	26.3			18.3	17.6
Amount per Withdrawal(Average £)	46	52			50	37	41	49	42			50	36
Counter Cheques Issued (1000s)	1.7	1.6			1.2	1.5	1.5	1.6	1.2			1.8	1.9
Digital													
Successful Logins (1000s)	107	87	101	95	102	98	65	76	87	170	145	78	90
Traffic to Website (1000s)	214	172	244	209	234	207	186	342	362	243	221	388	406
Peak user journey time (seconds)	12.0	15.3			18.7	20.3	17.6	15.2	16.9			17.0	18.4
Peak concurrent sessions (users)	190	198			150	298	187	205	389			147	231
Core IT													
Service status (reds)	0	10			0	0	0	0	0			0	0
Mainframe performance	97	87			88	95	84	82	81			87	86
Customer Operations													
Customer Telephone Calls (1000s)	16.8	18	11	6	19	17	16	17	19	11	7	20	5
Calls abandoned (%)	12.3	10.6	0.3	0.2	9.2	8.6	5.1	4.3	4.7	0.9	0.8	5.0	5.6
Account Closures	200	220			267	129	164	88	279			37	166
Total Faster Payments Outbound	75.0	38.0			101.0	68.0	64.0	78.0	81.0			90.0	94.0

Fig. 2.2: Dashboard 'Before'

Daily Flash Card
Reporting to 19th November 2013

Category	Metric	Avg of last month		Sat 09/11	Sun 10/11	Mon 11/11	Tue 12/11	Wed 13/11	Thu 14/11	Fri 15/11	Sat 16/11	Sun 17/11	Mon 18/11	Tue 19/11
Branches	Withdrawals Volume (£million)	19.6	15.9			31.7	17.6	15.6	17.9	26.3			18.3	17.6
	Amount per Withdrawal(Average £)	46	52			50	37	41	49	42			50	36
	Counter Cheques Issued (1000s)	1.7	1.6			1.2	1.5	1.5	1.6	1.2			1.8	1.9
Digital	Successful Logins (1000s)	107	87	101	95	102	98	65	76	87	170	145	78	90
	External Funds Transfers (Volume, 1000s)	14.75	14.4	9.2	8.8	13.7	12.7	11.9	11.9	16.5	9.5	9.2	14.2	12.6
	Traffic to Website (1000s)	214	172	244	209	234	207	186	342	362	243	221	388	406
	Peak user journey time (seconds)	12.0	15.3			18.7	20.3	17.6	15.2	16.9			17.0	18.4
	Peak concurrent sessions (users)	190	198			150	298	187	205	389			147	231
Core IT	Service status (reds)	0	10	0	0	0	0	0	0	0	0	0	0	0
	Mainframe performance	97	87			88	95	84	82	81			87	86
Customer Operations	Customer Telephone Calls (1000s)	16.8	18	11	6	19	17	16	17	19	11	7	20	5
	Calls abandoned (%)	12.3	10.6	0.3	0.2	9.2	8.6	5.1	4.3	4.7	0.9	0.8	5.0	5.6
	Account Closures	200	220			267	129	164	88	279			37	166
	Total Faster Payments Outbound	75.0	38.0			101.0	68.0	64.0	78.0	81.0		15.7	90.0	94.0

Maintained by: bernie.smith@madetomeasureKPIs.co.uk
Last updated: 22nd November 2013

Version number: 1.3

Fig. 2.3: Dashboard 'After'

Step 2 - Engage

Use KPI Trees to create a 'longlist' of measures

How to balance aspiration with practicality

There is always a tension between your ideal measures and the brutal reality of 'not enough resource', 'complexity' and 'practicality'. Often that tension can cloud managers' ability to think objectively about what the ideal set of KPIs might look like.

The approach to take is to first come up with the 'longlist', or the 'ideal-but-clearly-impractical' set of measures (this section) and then worry about the practicality and importance of each measure (the next section).

In this step, you are going to create a longlist of candidate measures that may be suitable for your dashboard or report. In the end you will not use **all** of the measures generated even though each one will be shown to link to your strategic objectives. One of your key tools is the 'KPI Tree'.

What is a KPI Tree?

A KPI Tree is a simple graphical tool to show the linkages between your strategic objectives and the things you measure on an everyday level.

Here is an example of a KPI Tree:

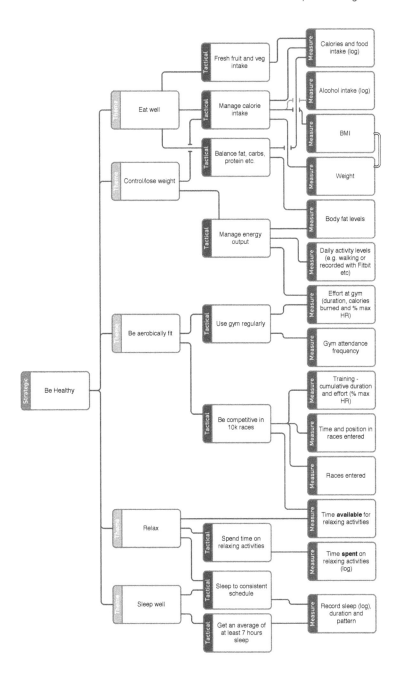

Fig. 3.1: An example KPI Tree for the strategic objective 'Be Healthy'

Key Idea

Why use a KPI Tree?

Most strategic objectives are high-level outcomes. It's very hard to agree with total confidence that you should, for example, measure 'process moisture content' as a way of delivering 'lowest cost per metre production of all manufacturers' unless you understand precisely how one links to the other.

There are a number of benefits that come from using KPI Trees.

Benefit 1 - Sum up a complex situation with just a few indicators

With the KPI Tree you naturally arrange sub-measures into meaningful groups. Creating high-level summary measures becomes relatively straightforward, as all you need to do is decide on the relative weightings and the arithmetic you use to blend the sub-measures.

Benefit 2 - Help build agreement

Every client I have worked with has featured a dominant character in the group. They can bounce a group into a particular set of measures through a mixture of rational argument and strength of will. Creating a KPI Tree avoids this through a highly collaborative series of sessions. It also gives a tool, structure and visible output that **anyone** can easily challenge and question.

Benefit 3 - Explain the approach

It normally takes two two-hour workshops to get a group up to speed and to successfully create a complex KPI Tree, but it's possible to get a group to grasp how to read one with about five minutes of explanation. It can also become a powerful way for the executive to explain their strategy in terms that a group can really understand. It shows a depth, coherence and clarity of thought that's rare when it comes to strategy and measures.

Benefit 4 - Keep in step with changes in strategy

Businesses, markets and executive teams change. It's absolutely guaranteed that, if you are lucky enough to have a good strategy, it will have to change - possibly very soon. Using the KPI Tree approach means that you can see what impact changes in the strategy will have on measures.

Benefit 5 - Understand how measures interact

You **can** have too much of a good thing. It's especially true in the world of measures. By pushing a 'good' measure too far you can unexpectedly have a negative impact on your ultimate strategic objective.

Going straight for the 'obvious' measure

Trap

One of my favourite examples of measures that interact is a measure used in call centres. Most of us have experienced a call centre agent who is clearly dying to get us off the line (even if they are scripted to hurriedly ask you 'Is there anything else I can help you with today, Mr Smith?'). The reason you can hear every sinew of their body pleading for you to get off the line is AHT. AHT, or 'Average Handling Time', is a measure that shows how long a call takes an agent to handle - on average. Note that it doesn't talk about whether the caller's objectives have been met, for example by resolving their problem or making sure it won't recur. AHT seems to make sense if you are running a big call-centre environment.

The logic goes 'I have lots of calls, so the quicker I can get through those calls the lower my wage bill will be and the shorter the queues will be.' Wrong. Pushing AHT reduction can rapidly increase call volumes. Agents become fixated with getting you off the phone at all costs. This leads to a decrease in 'first touch resolution' (the problem being sorted out, there and then, by the person who answers the phone) - as they will get you off the phone or pass you on to a colleague without resolving your problem themselves.

41

It's possible (even common) to see AHTs come down, but call volumes being driven up and customer satisfaction plummeting. The chances are that you have been fobbed off and passed around in call centres in the past and it may well be down to an 'apparently sensible' measure creating unexpected side effects.

Build out the branches of a KPI Tree

Below is a single branch from the earlier example, showing how you move progressively closer to something you can directly measure as you move towards the 'measures' level of the diagram.

Fig. 3.2: Drilling down one branch of the KPI Tree

As you go down the levels there is a one-to-many relationship. So, for example, our strategic objective 'Be healthy' has several enablers that link into it. Here are the enablers I've identified:

- Eat well
- Control/lose weight
- Be aerobically fit
- Relax
- Sleep well

Each of these will have several tactical enablers living below them, and measures below them. Here I have fleshed out the Eat well branch:

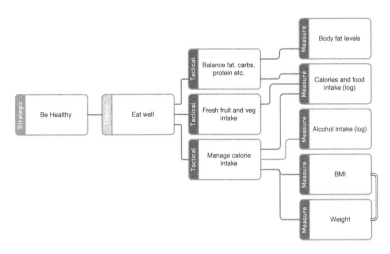

Fig. 3.3: Expanded branch of the KPI Tree

Any 'node' on the tree can be linked to any other to show a relationship. Use colour, intensity or terminator shape to distinguish between the three link types, described below.

Key Idea

Link 1 - Cause-effect

Where one activity directly influences another. This the most common type of relationship, so I use a plain grey line for this.

Examples of cause-effect relationships include:

- 'Sell popular flavours' causes 'Increase in ice cream sales'
- 'Consumption of free salty snacks' causes 'Increase in drinks sales'

43

Link 2 - Conflict

Where one activity conflicts with another. I use a red line to show this.

Examples of conflict relationships include:

- 'Minimise Average Handling Time' conflicts with 'Maximise First Touch Resolution'.
- 'Minimise performance rewards' conflicts with 'We have motivated staff'.

Link 3 - Companion

Where one measure is a subset of the other, or there is significant overlap. I use a double line for this - implying a two-way relationship.

Examples of companion relationships are:

- 'Weight' is a companion to 'Body Mass Index'.
- 'Reduce loss from car accidents' is a companion objective to 'Reduce injury from car accidents'.

How to build a KPI Tree

Build a KPI Tree: Preparation

Checklist

❏ Become fully familiar with the strategy of your organisation.

❏ Become fully familiar with the strategic objectives of your organisation.

❏ Double-check those strategic objectives with all engaged senior stakeholders - if there are differences then they **must** be ironed out before the sessions.

❏ Check that there are between two and seven strategic objectives - if there are more than this, it is likely that lower-level tactical objectives are in the mix.

❏ Gain support and approval to hold a session from senior stakeholder(s).

❏ Pull together some example outputs from previous sessions (or use the examples included in this book).

❏ Gather your stakeholders together in groups.

❏ Select groups of between three and nine people per session (certainly no more than twelve).

❏ Select group to have a good mix of seniority.

❏ Organise two two-hour long workshop sessions, separated by between one and five working days.

Practicalities

❏ Book meeting rooms for both sessions.

❏ Create briefing email and send out invitations.

❏ Base group selection around broadly similar remits.

❏ Make sure there are desks available for them to work at.

❏ Ensure a whiteboard is available, if possible.

❏ Print out examples and worksheets.

❏ Take Post-Its and pens to the session. A camera phone can also be useful.

Checklist

Build a KPI Tree: The first session

❏ Explain the approach.

❏ Identify the strategic objectives - agree these with the group.

❏ Give the background to the session.

❏ Show a finished example.

❏ Get the group to do a simple (non-work) exercise example.

❏ Explain the three link types: cause-effect, conflict and companion (see page 43).

❏ Help the group work through a more complex non-work example, including link types.

❏ Get the group to develop a draft KPI Tree specific to **the group's** relevant organisational strategic objectives.

❏ Develop one tree per objective. The trees will almost certainly cross-link so it makes sense to create them using one large sheet if possible.

Tip

If the participants start to get anxious about the number of potential measures this process is throwing up, then it's worth reassuring them that the whole point of this step is to generate the longlist of measures. You will absolutely **not** simply take this longlist and attempt to implement it as it stands at the end of this session. There is a critical next step which involves shortlisting candidate measures.

Follow-up work

❏ Write up the trees from all groups and merge into one tree.

❏ Add notes to show where decisions have had to be made on the merge.

Checklist

Build a KPI Tree: The second session

❏ Review the merged tree.

❏ Are there important factors that will not register with any of the measures identified? If so, then you have missed something out of your tree.

❏ Is there a way of making a measure go the 'right' way, but by doing something stupid?

❏ Add any further branches that need adding.

❏ Make corrections and discuss the merged tree.

The second session is normally quite straightforward as the group will be fresh, familiar with the purpose of the session and used to working as a group.

Follow up work

❏ Finish drawing up the trees from the second session (there may be several trees, but there should be only one version for each objective, the various versions having been merged after the first session).

❏ Add explanatory notes as needed.

❏ Circulate to the participants for final approval. State that the absence of a response will be taken as implicit approval.

Checklist

Tools for building KPI Trees

There are several choices for drawing diagrams. Key points you need to consider when choosing one are:

❏ Does the read/edit software have to be a standard desktop application (like Microsoft Word or PowerPoint) or do you have the chance to install specialist applications like Visio or Aris?

❏ What is the IT skill level of the users?

47

❏ Do you have to attach meta-data to objects? If so, you will need to go for a more specialist diagram package e.g. Visio.

❏ Is there a company standard currently in use for this type of diagram? E.g. Mindjet, mind mapping software.

❏ Will the software be used on a variety of operating systems? Some applications like OpenOffice, Freemind and Mindjet cover two or more operating systems. Others, such as Visio, tie you firmly to one platform.

❏ What level of annotation and general sophistication are you looking for? How many nodes/branches do you need to fit in?

How to fit complex KPI Trees on one page

Although people generally like brightly coloured diagrams, the most space-efficient method is a wire tree diagram as shown in fig. 3.4 on the next page. This style, championed by Jon Moon in 'How to Make an Impact', often takes 5-10 times fewer pages than the same data represented in an 'organisation chart' style KPI Tree. The example wire tree was done entirely within Excel, mostly using the 'Borders' function. An additional benefit of this approach is that you can add lots of supporting data to each KPI in cells off to the right of the tree.

You can download a wire tree template from my website using this shortlink: **http://wp.me/p1H6XP-zD**

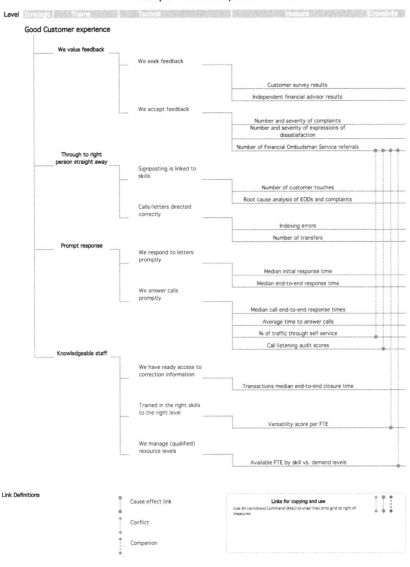

Fig. 3.4: A much more space-efficient way of showing KPI relationships. This diagram was produced using Excel.

Tip

Tools to consider if you prefer 'Mind Map' style diagrams

If you like the slightly more chaotic 'Mind Map' style of diagram, other tools that are worth considering for KPI Trees are:

- Visio (PC)
- Word/PowerPoint Draw Tools (PC, Mac)
- Omnigraffle (Mac)
- SmartDraw (PC)
- Lucid (Web app, multi-platform)
- MindMeister (Web app, free)
- Mindjet MindManager (Mac, PC)
- Xmind (PC, Mac) free
- FreeMind (Java) free
- IMindMap (PC, Mac, Linux)

Develop the measures 'shortlist'

Key Idea

The shortlisting method

By the time you have created your KPI Tree(s) you will have a large number of candidate measures. Some teams are horrified when they realise that they have come up with 70, 80 or more measures. The good news is that you definitely won't use all of the measures that you have on your KPI Tree.

Reasons for not including the measures would include:

- The measure isn't important enough.
- It's just not physically possible to measure or report on it.
- You will report on it, but it's going to require more work or time to do it.

How to cut the measures that don't really count

Your next task is to reduce that list. You will do this by getting the group to rate each measure on two criteria, **Importance** and **Availability**, and plot those ratings on a four box grid or matrix.

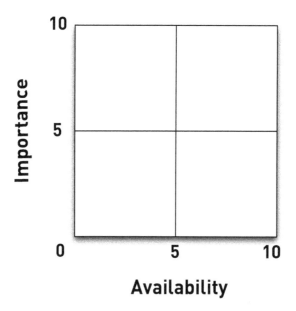

Fig. 4.1: An example blank KPI shortlisting matrix

Here is a bit more description on those two criteria:

Importance: Is the measure significant to your business?

This is not normally a yes/no choice, but it's usually possible to get a group to rank importance on a 0-10 scale. Importance can be broken down into criticality and breadth-of-influence if you are having real problems agreeing, although I've never had to go this far in real life. 10 is the maximum importance rating here.

Availability: How easy is it to get hold of the data?

10, the 'most available' score, would be information that is automatically-generated, fully trusted and can be sliced and diced in whichever way you choose with little or no effort.

0 means that the data is effectively unavailable, requiring unrealistic levels of effort and disruption to collect it. In some circumstances it may not be physically possible to collect this information at all.

True Story

Measuring the unmeasurable

It is quite common in manufacturing process industries to be unable to measure a process parameter directly without 'breaking' the process you are trying to measure. In that situation you will often measure the direct drivers of that parameter, knowing that if they are under control then the process variable you are interested in will be under control as well.

For example, in paper making you have a very thin, very fragile sheet of paper forming on a machine which moves at high speed. Physically measuring the thickness of the sheet without stopping the process is virtually impossible, so you actually measure the absorption rate of gamma radiation, from a calibrated source, and calculate the thickness based on that absorption.

So the key with anything that is 'unmeasurable' is to look at something that either **affects** or is **affected by** the thing you are interested in.

Another example of this is judging how interested toddlers are in a TV programme by seeing how frequently they are distracted by a pile of interesting toys. This is the technique used by the creators of Sesame Street to gauge how absorbing each element of their show was.

Checklist

KPI shortlisting process checklist

❏ Firstly, make sure you are dealing with actual measures (the lowest-level boxes on the KPI Tree), not the higher-level headings.

❏ Get a flip chart.

❏ Label **Importance** on the vertical axis and **Availability** on the horizontal axis.

❏ Number the bottom-level measures on your KPI Tree for reference. I haven't done this in the examples, but it is a good way of staying on top of things.

❏ Add dividing lines at the midpoint of each axis so that you have a grid of four boxes or matrix.

❏ Go through each candidate measure with the group rating it on a scale of 0-10 for:

  • Importance

  • Availability

❏ Note down any disagreements about the scores the group assigns - this can be useful if you are challenged later on the choices made, and it gives you an audit trail.

❏ Plot each candidate measure on the chart, with a cross and the measure name (or number).

You should end up with something that looks like this..

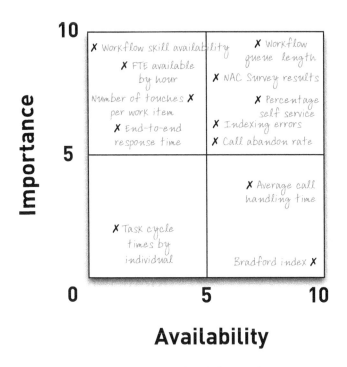

Fig. 4.2: An example populated KPI shortlisting matrix

Tip

Using Post-it notes for each measure can give you flexibility if there is debate about the rating for each KPI. Just make sure you take a picture of the flip **before** you take it down as you can lose a lot of work if your notes fall off!

How to use the matrix

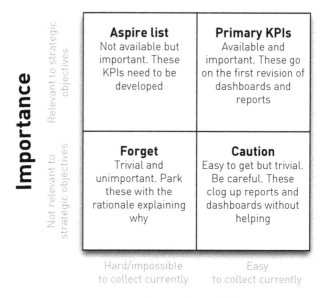

Fig. 4.3: What each quadrant means

Top right-hand box - The high-importance and easily available quadrant is the tranche of measures you put on your first dashboard/report. Easy to get and important, why wouldn't you?

Top left-hand box - The high-importance and difficult-to-collect quadrant. The Aspire list becomes the 'to-do' list for your dashboard. This is where you focus your KPI development effort.

Bottom right-hand box - These are the trivial but easy to collect measures. It is worth double-checking any that border on important, but don't get sucked into putting something on the dashboard or report simply because you can.

Bottom left-hand box - The trivial and yet hard-to-collect measures. Unless these are close to the centre of the quadrant boundaries, forget these and move on. If they are close to the top right-hand box you may just want to double-check your assessment.

By the end of the session you should have divided your candidate measures into three:

- Do-it-straight-away list of measures - the **Use** list
- To-do list of measures to develop - the **Aspire** list
- Rejected measures (with reasons) - the **Discard** list

Tip

Why the Discard list is important

It is easy to overlook the last point, as you are not going to implement these measures, but that would be a mistake. Recording which measures you chose to reject with the reasons why can be a really powerful way of defending the choices made. 'We didn't go with that measure and here are the reasons why...' can be powerful in stopping report 'bloat' and demonstrating the rigour of the process.

Develop measures to fill the gaps - Your Aspire list measures

The measures that ended up in the Aspire list may just not be measured currently or they may be important but tricky to measure.

Although in some situations it may be easy to add the new measures into existing data collection systems, very often it isn't that straightforward. I would recommend setting up each measure as a 'mini project'. This gives you some framework and structure and stops you potentially sleepwalking into something nasty.

Checklist

Develop your missing measures and KPIs

❑ Confirm that you do really want to measure this thing/these things.

❑ Identify stakeholders (using the RACI matrix approach from Step 2, page 28).

❑ Define the measure (using the KPI definition sheet in the next chapter).

❑ Review that definition with the key stakeholders.

❑ Do a quick feasibility study - especially if there's IT involved.

❑ Check to see what organisational project management methods and systems you need to fit in with.

❑ Assign a full-time or part-time project manager.

❑ Put together a one-page 'charter'. A charter is a short document that outlines objectives, resources, timescales and anticipated issues (with mitigations).

❑ Draft a simple project plan.

❑ Review the timescale and cost - are you still sure you want to go ahead?

❑ Create and maintain an action log.

❑ Set up some simple project governance (e.g. rules, meeting schedule etc.) to make sure the project stays on track.

In some cases it may be more substantial than a 'small' project but the principles remain the same and there's plenty of guidance out there for running projects.

Action logs are simple but useful tools to keep things on track. You can download a free template for one the I've built in Excel by following this shortlink: **http://wp.me/p1H6XP-zD**

Of course, you can easily create your own. If you do, make sure you have the following covered:

Checklist

Track actions

❏ A unique reference number for each action.

❏ A grouping description, if it's a long list, like 'IT' or 'Training'.

❏ A meaningful description of the action.

❏ Who owns the action.

❏ When the action is due by.

❏ When the action is closed.

❏ Whether the action is on hold.

❏ Any relevant notes or comments.

❏ Risks (optional).

❏ Mitigations (optional).

Step 4 - Shortlist KPIs

Define KPIs and meeting inputs

Key Idea

Define your KPIs

If there's one simple tool that you can put into action today that will dramatically improve the quality of your KPIs and add a stack of professional credibility to your reputation, this is it. What I'm about to describe may sound very obvious and simple, but that doesn't make it any less useful or powerful.

An issue that almost every business seems to have is what I call the 'common sense' problem. What I mean by this is that many KPIs and measures use descriptive names. This can be very dangerous as the human mind has a tendency to make assumptions based on the name.

Let's take an example. There is a very common operational measure called 'utilisation'. It is often used by professional services firms to show what proportion of the available employee time was used for billed work to the client. It's an important measure, and one that is used across a number of industries.

So here's a plain English definition: 'Utilisation is the ratio of billed hours to available hours for an individual.'

That seems pretty simple, doesn't it? But let's look at some of the questions that this does not answer:

- By available hours do you mean nominal or actual and do you include overtime?
- What about holidays or sickness absence, is that zero utilisation?
- By individual do you mean only individuals who are billable, or do you include support staff?
- Do you include mandatory commitments, such as safety training, in the available hours?
- What about sales? This is clearly a value-add activity but is not billable.
- What happens if you bill at a much reduced hourly rate?

Does that utilisation count the same as full-rate work?

- What do you do with staff who have dual roles, only one of which is a billable position?

Clearly there is plenty of scope for misunderstanding here. It's pretty rare to find a plain English definition that does not give rise to lots of similar questions. So what's the way around this? It's a KPI definition database. When I say database I mean it in the loosest sense of the word. It could just be a Word document or an Excel spreadsheet. The important thing is that you record a really clear description of precisely what is being measured, where, how and when.

So on the next page are the questions that need to be answered for each and every KPI to help you avoid this kind of confusion.

KPI definition

Checklist

❏ **KPI name:** Use a 'what-it-says-is-what-it-is' type name, so that it doesn't mislead. Be very careful with terms like 'efficiency' and 'effectiveness' – there are lots of variants on these and everyone will have a strong view that their usage is the right one.

❏ **Measurement intent:** Describes the measure and the reasoning behind its selection as an indicator of progress against a strategic objective. Put simply 'Why are you measuring this?'

❏ **KPI definition/formula:** Provides a detailed formula for the calculation of a numeric value for the measure. A simple test for how well you have defined a KPI is to pose the question 'Could a reasonably numerate stranger calculate the value using this definition and relevant source data?'

❏ **Frequency of update:** Identifies how often it's calculated. This is important for a number of reasons, one of the less obvious ones being 'end effects', where the reporting cycle may create some overlap errors. A long reporting cycle usually lessens these while a short one will make this more acute.

❏ **Units of measure:** Identifies the units in which the measure will be reported. Is it a dimensionless ratio (e.g. efficiency) or is it a good old-fashioned 'real' measure with dimensions (e.g. kilograms, money or calls per day)?

❏ **Notes/Assumptions:** Clarifies terms used and highlights key assumptions within the formula. Almost all measures and KPIs have flaws, issues and problems. The key thing is to document these issues, make people aware of them and avoid making flawed analyses based on these issues.

❏ **KPI information availability:** Whether the information required is: readily available, available with some effort or not available. This gives you a feeling for the pain involved in compiling a KPI and can give you a 'hit list' for automating and streamlining KPI production.

❏ **Data elements and source:** The data elements required to calculate this measure and the source systems, databases, documents etc. of those data elements. This should go down to painful levels of detail showing on which server a file sits, in which directory and where on the spreadsheet the data can be found. Naming conventions should also be included where documents cover a certain period.

❏ **Target (where known)**: What is the target value?

❏ **Source for, and approach to, setting targets:** Where does the target come from? Why is it set at the level it is? I've seen countless organisations where no one can answer this question. Why are you aiming for a certain score? It's pretty embarrassing not to know the answer to this.

❏ **Person responsible for target setting:** One person must ultimately be responsible for setting the target, even if it's agreed by consensus/debate/vote.

❏ **Person accountable for set targets:** This is the person who carries the 'strategic can' for the target setting. They should be consulted on the target and its aims, but may not be responsible for setting its actual value.

❏ **Person responsible for tracking and reporting targets:** Who manages the day-to-day process of target setting and reporting?

Each of these questions needs to be answered for each KPI and measure in the organisation. Tedious? Yes. Important? Also, yes. The definitions should be held in a single managed location so that multiple definitions don't coexist. This will avoid confusion and arguments.

The benefits of this kind of document are:

- It forces your organisation to clarify and discuss the KPI definitions.
- Any weakness or uncertainty around a KPI is written down and 'out in the open'.
- You avoid having similar sounding (or identical) KPIs or measures that are actually calculated in different ways.
- It is a reference document for people who are unclear or uncertain how a measure is calculated.

You can download the KPI Definition template from my website using this shortlink **http://wp.me/p1H6XP-zD**

Measure/KPI Name

Measure name

Measure/KPI Name ref. number

Unique code for i.d.

Measurement intent

Describe what outcome this measure is linked to.

Frequency of update

How often is the KPI produced? Daily, weekly, monthly etc.

Units of measure

Percentage, hours, count etc

Data elements and sources

What are the data sources? Detail this right down to where a source spreadsheet is located, which tab and in which column which the data is located. It should be sufficiently detailed to allow a novice to locate the data unassisted.

KPI data availability

Is it automatically generated or does it require high levels of manual input? Is substantial data cleansing part of the production process?

KPI production owner

Name and contact details here

KPI Definition/Formula

A precise description, including formula and calculations.

Notes and assumptions

What issues are there with the data? Are there situations in which there are known limitations or errors?

KPI targets

Target

Describe what outcome this measure is linked to.

Source for, and approach to, setting targets

On what basis is the target set? An assessment of what's physically possible, an arbitrary percentage increase/decrease?

Person accountable for targets set

Name here

Person responsible for tracking and reporting targets

Name here

Person responsible for target setting

Name here

Reporting the KPI

Person Accountable

Name here

Person Responsible

Name here

People Consulted

Names here

People Informed

Names here

Driving the performance behind the KPI

Person Accountable

Name here

Person Responsible

Name here

People Consulted

Names here

People Informed

Names here

Fig. 5.1: A sample KPI Definition Worksheet template

Set up meetings that work

Most meetings should centre on decisions based on good information and analysis. The reports and dashboards you will be prototyping in the next step should feed those meetings with the right information. Without being absolutely clear on what a meeting is for, you have little chance of supplying the right reports and dashboards.

You need to know precisely what reporting input is required for your meetings. This is done through a meeting's 'Terms of Reference' or TOR, normally a one-page document outlining the inputs, outputs and objectives of a meeting. The checklist on the next page goes into a little bit more detail. There is also a simple template over the page.

As meetings are such a key part of making good use of KPIs (and are often so dreadful) I have put some extra checklists on meetings in the Appendix.

You can download the Terms of Reference template shown on the next page from: **http://wp.me/p1H6XP-zD**

Term of Reference for:

Purpose and scope:	Attendees:		Medium: Delete as applicable Face to face Telecon Telepresence Desktop video
Chair(s):	Planned duration:	Frequency:	Location:
Agenda		Meeting input data and reports	
		Owners responsible for supply of input data and reports	
Meeting outputs (decisions, approvals, actions etc.)		Agreed SLA for supply of input data and reports	

Terms of Reference maintained by _____ , contact details

Fig. 5.2: A sample meetings' Terms of Reference template

The basics for a meeting's Terms of Reference

Checklist

❏ What is the purpose of the meeting?

❏ What is the scope of the meeting? Which part of the organisation, approval level etc.

❏ What are the inputs for the meeting? Data, reports, samples etc.

❏ When should the attendees get reports and documents prior to the meeting - i.e. what is the SLA for production of these documents?

❏ What are the outputs of the meeting? E.g. Decisions, budget approval, judgements, sign-off etc.

❏ Who should be there? By role and authority.

❏ Is there clear guidance on the use of deputies and their authority?

❏ How often does the meeting happen?

❏ Who runs the meeting? By role. If you need to put names in there then make sure you have contingency owners as well.

❏ What are the roles and responsibilities? E.g. Minute taking, organisation, producing the timetable etc.

❏ Where does the meeting happen?

❏ How long is the meeting?

❏ How do you change the Terms of Reference - who do you contact?

You should summarise this in a one-page document and circulate to the proposed meeting attendees for sign-off. I like to use a simple template like the one in fig. 5.2 to keep things consistent.

Go live with a meeting's Terms of Reference

The most effective way to implement a new Terms of Reference is gently but persistently. As a rule, 'big bang' introductions don't work for very long and are quickly forgotten. It requires sustained reinforcement to get people to modify their behaviour. The Chair is in the best position to exert this sustained pressure, so they need to be up to the job.

Prototype your dashboards and reports

Why prototype?

It is quite rare to find a client (internal or external) who knows precisely what they want from a dashboard or report. If you catch them with no preparation they will normally reach for an existing report and tell you which bits they want changing and moving. Sometimes this ends with them sighing in a frustrated way as they realise just how far from 'ideal' the current report is and they become overwhelmed by the scale of the challenge.

The solution is to create prototypes collaboratively with your internal customer. This takes some care and thought as they are not usually report design specialists.

What is prototyping?

Prototyping means building non-working or partially working examples of the end product - reports and dashboards in your case. Doing this can avoid massive amounts of wasted effort. Even with a good prototype process you may go through 5-10 design iterations. If you build and modify fully working reports over every iteration it can take a long time and waste large amounts of developer/analyst resource (and it's not much fun either).

Even prototyping needs some groundwork to be done. I have discovered that, in some situations, the current poor report design was a direct result of the design choices made in the prototyping session. To avoid repeating the same mistakes you need to agree some good design principles. To make this work the principles need to be backed up by some real science and research.

How to prototype dashboards and reports

Stage 1: Discuss and agree the principles of good design

Make sure that you won't be proposing Sparklines (the most simplified type of graph there is) and utter minimalism when your client is craving multi-coloured backgrounds and painstakingly rendered gauge widgets like this:

This is a tricky conversation as many senior clients have strong views on this. It's best to stick to evidence. Fortunately there's lots of evidence to say that extreme restraint in the presentation of data leads to better understanding. To look at this in much more depth you could also read BlinkReporting, my book on exactly this topic.

See 'Train stakeholders in quantitative visual presentation techniques' on page 32 for more details and a half price voucher.

Tip

Stage 2: Watch how the current reports and dashboards are really used

Observation will normally give you good insight into how people currently use information (if at all):

- Ask people how they currently use their reports.
- Sit in on the relevant meetings and watch how they are actually used.
- Look for any differences between what you observed and what you were told.

If there are big differences then proceed with caution. It suggests there is a 'reality gap', which may mean that your final product succumbs to the same fate as the previous report or dashboard. It may be that you are seeing a behavioural rather than a reporting issue here. With behavioural problems, changing the documentation will not fix the underlying problems.

Stage 3: Create design options

Decision-makers always respond well to mocked-up options. Whilst it may be hard for them to explain what they want without anything in front of them, suddenly it becomes a matter of pointing to the one they prefer when presented with a range of options. Design features will also trigger valuable discussions.

There are three basic approaches used in prototyping:

Option 1 Create a number of versions 'off-line' and present them to your key decision-makers.

Option 2 Build a dashboard in a live collaborative session with your key decision-makers.

Option 3 Use the first approach to create some options then hold a live session to adjust and tune them.

Option 1 is the lowest risk, but also the slowest. If you have a customer who is prone to changing his mind or likes a lot of options it can be easy to get bogged down with this approach.

Option 2 works well if you have a patient decision-maker who is happy to get involved. You will also need to be very proficient in your chosen prototyping tool (Visio or Excel, for example). Often building a template or stencil, specific to your purpose, can speed things up. I have a set of stock charts - in my preferred presentational style - with dummy data ranges, set up for prototyping sessions. I also have an Excel data sheet with dummy data ranges showing a variety of trends with realistic scatter. This type of session takes time and is sensitive to IT issues, so make sure you are set up properly and have a contingency plan in case things go wrong (like a projector bulb blowing) - even if it's just a whiteboard, markers and a camera phone.

Option 3 is the approach I prefer to use. You present some pre-prepared designs, but tune and tweak them with the decision-maker **in** a session. This seems to achieve the best balance between efficient time usage and rapid design prototyping.

Stage 4 (optional): Review and score existing reports and dashboards

If there is disagreement over the quality of the existing reports and documentation, a good way to assess the current quality is to use a design review checklist. It can take some of the emotion out of the discussion and help build consensus on the need for action. It is best to run a training session on design principles first.

If running a training session is not possible then reading a good book is the next best thing. Of course, I'd recommend my book - BlinkReporting (see page 32), but I would also take the time to read Stephen Few's book 'Information Dashboard Design'. If you want something a bit broader, but more academic, then take a look a Edward Tufte's classic text 'The Visual Display of Quantitative Information' (See page 175 for the Bibliography).

Once you have run the training, encourage some key stakeholders to critique their own reports. I will often use client-specific examples during the training (just take care not to cause too much embarrassment).

The following design checklist encourages you to consider each element of your design and to score it. You can use the score to objectively show the **improvement** to a document (although ultimately this is a subjective thing). It is pretty long, at 53 questions, but it does cover most areas of design. With practice you will probably not need to refer to this list but it can be a useful memory jogger. It gives a semi-objective framework that can take some of the emotion out of critiquing existing dashboards and reports.

Demo Donuts Dashboard

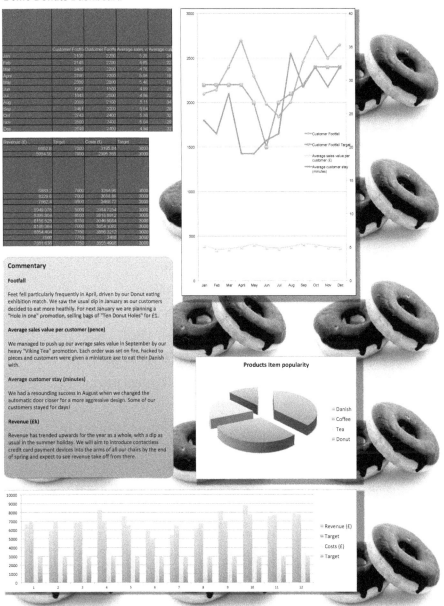

Fig. 6.1: An example dashboard that breaks pretty much every rule of good design. Use it alongside the questions to spot the problems.

Checklist

Review existing reports and dashboards - The Brilliant Dashboards Checklist

Question scoring: 1=poor, 5=good

Visual design

❏ Is colour used to convey additional information?

❏ Are colours used consistently for the same meaning?

❏ Is a consistent design theme used for all charts and text boxes?

❏ Are there unnecessary boxes and dividers?

❏ Do dividers and boxes lead the eye in a helpful way?

❏ With RAG (red-amber-green 'traffic light') indicators, is it clear what criteria are used for RAG?

❏ Are there unnecessary tick marks?

❏ Are there unnecessary borders on chart areas?

❏ Is the background unnecessarily shaded?

❏ Are the columns/bars unnecessarily shaded?

❏ Are there unnecessary borders on columns?

Layout

❏ Are text and chart size proportionate to the importance of the information being conveyed?

❏ Are data points that need comparison near to each other?

❏ Are logos and ornamentation kept to a bare minimum?

❏ Is spacing consistent and pleasing?

❏ Are lines used to guide the eye in a meaningful direction?

❏ Is there a 'logical hierarchy' for text and comments?

Structure

❏   Are there large amounts of numbers that need to be read to understand the high-level situation?

❏   Can you quickly navigate to the section of the report you need?

❏   Is it clear where the biggest issues are and how to navigate to find more information?

❏   Are targets clearly different from data sets?

Charts

❏   Do the graphs and charts meet your objectives?

❏   Are the charts intuitive i.e. no need for careful study or explanation?

❏   Do the charts have impact and give insight? Do the charts allow meaningful comparison of relevant data sets?

❏   Do charts clearly show patterns and trends?

❏   Does understanding the document tax your short-term memory too much?

❏   Do your eyes have to leap about the page to understand the document?

❏   Do the charts answer an obvious question?

❏   If the chart uses 3D, is 3D actually required to represent the information?

❏   Is the message clear?

Axes

❏   Are the axes 'fair' and labelled? Unfair axes might include logarithmic axes that are not clearly indicated or axes that are not clearly marked as starting from a value other than zero.

❏   Are the fonts clear, the right size and readable?

❏ If you use a double axis, is it required to make a valid point?

Labelling

❏ Are all charts clearly labelled, avoiding jargon or acronyms?

❏ Is it clear what period the charts refer to?

❏ Are labels physically near to the things they are describing?

❏ If unavoidable, is jargon defined?

❏ Is the level of labelling appropriate or is it obscuring the chart (or the message)?

❏ Are numbers on the chart given to realistic precision (i.e. not to 5 decimal places if that precision is inappropriate for the accuracy of the source data)?

Trending

❏ Is there meaningful trending?

❏ Are gridlines aiding or obscuring clarity?

❏ Is there unhelpful use of colour and area/fill patterns?

Text

❏ Is the text relevant?

❏ Is the text concise?

❏ Is the text spelled correctly and without grammatical errors?

❏ Is it clear with which graph any text is associated?

❏ Is any additional text clear, the right size and readable?

Visual clarity

❏ Is the document (and its sub-elements) an optimal size?

❏ Does the layout work for the delivery medium?

   E.g. a smartphone, iPad or projector?

❏ Do any of your intended audience have eyesight issues? If so, is the output of suitable size, colour and contrast?

Other points on appearance and readability

❏ It is possible to understand the general message 'at a glance'?

❏ Is it clear who created the report and contents?

❏ Is it clear who to talk to if there's a query or correction and how to contact them?

On the next page you can see the same data reworked using the 'BlinkReporting' approach (the checklist and examples are from my book of the same name).

The example may not be very 'pretty', but my clients have told me over and over that this style becomes very clear and easy to understand - particularly with familiarity.

Demo Donuts Dashboard

Fig. 6.2: The same data as in fig. 6.1, reworked using the BlinkReporting approach. Dull, at first glance, but much more understandable.

Approve your revised designs

If you don't want to get the prototype designs into production only to have to completely revise them again, it's essential to get the final design approved by the relevant stakeholders.

The best way to do this is:

- Identify stakeholders using a RACI matrix (see 'Identify stakeholder types and groups' on page 27 for how to do this) to identify the correct stakeholders and agree a sign-off plan with the person identified as 'Accountable' on the matrix.
- Agree a sign-off schedule to avoid endless revision sessions.
- Make sure there is a final arbiter so that there is no 'tug of war' between stakeholders.
- Get the approvers to put their approval **in writing**.

Step 6 - Prototype

Roll out your KPIs, reports and dashboards

Get buy-in

Using the phrase 'buy-in' is probably putting it a bit strongly. For many KPI implementations the best you're looking for initially is the absence of resistance and compliance in terms of gathering information.

Proper buy-in normally only comes after people start to see real value coming from the data. There are a few situations, such as particularly acute, highly visible or painful problems, where it is straightforward to build enthusiasm right from the word go.

We can divide buy-in into five stages:

- Creating engagement.
- Building a case - why you need these measures.
- Removing obstructions.
- Public displays of importance.
- Developing good habits.

Checklist

Create engagement

❏   Involve a wide selection of stakeholders in the KPI Tree session. Of all the points on this list this is probably the most effective way of building engagement.

❏   Go through the reasons behind the new measures clearly and simply with those who are providing the data or are being measured.

❏   Hold an event, or series of one-to-ones, in which people can frankly and honestly discuss concerns and issues with the proposed measures.

❏   Deal with potential issues openly and honestly.

❏   Create a 'frequently asked questions' document for those that could not be involved in the initial engagement process.

Build a case

It's rational to start by explaining to the team that you need to measure X because if you don't you are going to 'go bust', 'upset customers' or 'get into trouble with the regulators' etc. Here are the typical steps you would go through to build a 'rational' case:

Checklist

Build the case for measurement

❏ Show that there is a real-world benefit from collecting the data. Alternatively, show that there is a significant problem that will arise or become worse if you don't do this.

❏ Give relevant and compelling real-life examples of the problems that will be tackled or solved through this approach.

❏ Explain how you will manage the practicalities of the extra workload created through data collection or analysis.

Whilst this does need to be done, this alone will not build engagement. Engagement is essentially an emotional process and you have just outlined a rational argument.

The best way to build buy-in is to start with emotional engagement followed by a KPI Tree mapping session or stakeholder feedback workshop.

It's not a straightforward thing, but emotional engagement needs the following in place to work:

- Honesty during dialogue.
- Trust between both parties.
- People to be listened to and **feel** that they are being listened to.
- Small group (or one-to-one) conversations.
- Relevancy to the needs of the person you are talking to.

A frequent mistake managers make is to react to a lack of engagement by strengthening the rational argument for 'the case'. Winning the intellectual argument does not bring people on board emotionally. In fact, steamrollering people with rational argument can often have a completely counter-productive effect.

Remove obstructions

This is about making life as easy as possible for those that you want to deliver the data or analyses. There is research to show that the easier you make things, the more likely people are to do them.

Checklist

Make it easy to comply with the new system

❏ Create a user-guide for each type of user that will be recording or manipulating data.

❏ Clearly define the process that you want the person or team to follow.

❏ Test that process with all of the individuals who will be following it, if possible.

Checklist

Create a simple user guide document by:

❏ Making it easy to use
  • Step-by-step instructions.
  • Decision branches.
  • On-screen instructions or screen grabs.

❏ Identify additional required user skills and where to acquire those skills.

❏ Contact details for additional help - the more immediate the better. A telephone number is great, having to write a letter is not!

❏ Make the user guides readily available and easy-to-use.

❏ Laminated, colour, A3 user-guides work brilliantly.

❏ Make sure the guides are version-controlled and fully

up to date. Ensure that changes to the user-guides are actioned as fast as humanly possible.

❏ Take on board any feedback as quickly as possible - nothing kills the process quicker than lack of interest from its advocates.

Make sure that the line managers of your key data gatherers are fully engaged and are banging the drum for the new system. Any dissent among these people, however subtle, will absolutely destroy your efforts to collect new measures. However tempting it is to bypass middle managers, avoid it at all costs!

Checklist

Keep people engaged

❏ Make it easy for people to highlight problems.

❏ Create a 30-second 'any issues session' in the morning operational meeting, if it exists.

❏ Add a 'comments and improvements' box on frequently used documentation.

❏ Spend some time sitting with people as they collect and record any data that you are requesting. (This does a couple of things. It makes it easier for them to highlight problems and also shows that there is a keen interest in the data that is being collected.)

❏ Let people know quickly about any actions taken as the result of feedback. If you can't address feedback positively, let people know why.

Public displays of importance

No, this doesn't mean having a special KPI hat that teams need to wear. This is about making sure that both the tangible and intangible signals being delivered by senior management are positive and supportive of the KPI process. You need to do your homework beforehand, because discovering that you have no support at this point can be very embarrassing and frustrating.

Checklist

Test support for the implementation

❏ Have full and frank discussions with the senior managers right at the start to make sure that they are fully engaged and supportive.

❏ Document what it is you're trying to achieve and get them to sign it off (and, yes, I mean **physically** sign it off).

❏ Get your senior stakeholders to write a briefing document explaining why this is so important. If you can't get them to do this (due to the usual 'I'm too busy', 'I don't have my diary' or 'Could you do me a favour and write one for me?'), then you will need to write one for them to sign off. Not ideal but better than nothing.

❏ Ensure that senior stakeholders kick off any roadshow, frequently asked questions or roll-out briefing sessions. They need to explain:

- Why it's important.
- What will happen if it doesn't succeed.
- The interest they will show in this.
- When the next follow-up is.
- What they will expect to see in a follow-up.
- Their confidence in the success of this process.

❏ Let people know there is an open door to discuss any real and practical problems that may come up.

❏ Make sure that everything the senior stakeholders say in public and private is aligned and supportive of what you're trying to do.

❏ Private off-the-record comments are often taken very seriously by subordinates and if you're hearing whispers that are not aligned to the project objectives you need to address these very seriously and as early as possible.

❏ Follow-up here is really important so schedule in regular review or 'steering' sessions to keep everybody focused.

Tip

Developing good habits

Good habits can be really helpful with a new KPI system. Habits take time to form. Once people have got into the habit of gathering and analysing the data that you need, things get a lot easier. In the same way that you barely think about cleaning your teeth in the morning, so people will start to semi-automatically produce and process the information that your KPI system depends upon.

There's an awful lot of pseudo-science around the number of repetitions required to form a habit. I'm not going to try and come up with the 'magic figure' for habit formation but you will certainly recognise when you reach that stage. When you reach that stage, things get done as part of everyday business, rather than as the result of chasing. There are certain things that you can do to help habit formation - or to really stuff it up.

Checklist

Make sure data collection stays on track

❏ Minimise the amount of process variation between repetitions. Don't make the process too different each time if you can possibly avoid it.

❏ Make sure there is a 'heartbeat' i.e. a predictable frequency between repetitions.

❏ Tackle any instances of 'falling out of the habit' as quickly as possible.

❏ Fix any problems that stop people doing what they should - and fast!

❏ Reinforce good work with plenty of positive feedback. Track and measure errors and omissions on a visual management chart, if practicable and appropriate.

Trap

Things to avoid..

❏ Changing the process frequently or unnecessarily.

❏ Changing the layout or position of user interfaces, forms or documentation.

❏ Making the process complex, cumbersome or difficult to adhere to.

❏ Allowing 'grey' exceptions to exist without clear guidance on procedure. This will only encourage people to park something not completed.

How to deal with existing data and its problems

Something that commonly derails a management control system is the practicality of actually collecting the data. It is worth dividing the problems into separate categories because the solutions vary according to the type of problem.

Typical data problems and solutions

The five most common problems are:

Problem 1 - Data living in small 'islands' in spreadsheets, Word documents and ad hoc databases around the organisation.

Problem 2 - Datasets containing contradictory information, leading to terminal indecision over which dataset is valid and which one to use.

Problem 3 - Data existing in different forms.

Problem 4 - Lack of trust in the data.

Problem 5 - Large delays in the collection and collation of the data.

Over the next few pages I'll outline what the problems look like and methods for tackling them.

Problem 1 - Data living in small islands

This is fairly simple to spot but probably the toughest of challenges to resolve.

Dealing with stranded islands of data
- Develop a clear definition of which unique KPIs you need to collect.
- Create a production process map for the measure (see 'Map KPI production' on page 133 for how to do this).

This process should quickly flush out any ambiguity over where the data comes from and concerns over its accuracy. The beauty of this approach is it involves talking to almost everyone in the data supply chain, so you find out lots of really useful incidental information.

Tip

Showing where data lives in the organisation

Create a simple table like the example below, showing the data grouped by where it is stored.

Data	Use	Storage method	Location	Source or duplicate?	Owner	Contact details
Mortgage book	Exec report	Spreadsheet from database extract	MI team Sharepoint. MExecRep directory	Extract from Oracle dbase ref. k27	Laura Pringle	ext. 4555 l.pringle@ac mebank.com
Liquidity	Exec report	Spreadsheet	Risk team, shared directory xxx	Source	Jamie Walker	ext. 7524 j.walker@ac mebank.com
Complaints	Exec report	Emailed spreadsheet	Jim's directory, MI team	Duplicate	Jim Dorito	ext. 1744 j.dorito@acm ebank.com

Fig. 7.1: A table showing where data lives and whether it is duplicated

Then answer each of these three questions:

- Is this the right place to store this information?
- Is the method by which this information is collected clearly defined and effective?
- Is there a better method for moving that information from the storage point to the point of use, in a hassle-free and reliable way?

It may be that the most practical solution to your problem still involves emailing spreadsheets, faxing bits of paper and ringing around with some numbers. The truth is that this can still be a reasonably effective system so long as it is managed carefully and documented. A simple template for this can be downloaded from my website: **http://wp.me/p1H6XP-zD**

Problem 2 - Datasets containing contradictory information

This is a common problem and can rapidly undermine management confidence in the KPI system. Even someone who knows nothing about measurement knows that if you look at, say, a figure for widget production in July 2007, then you would expect any other figures for widget production in July 2007 to be the same, wouldn't you? So if they are exposed to similar-looking measures that give contradictory or differing figures, it shakes that person's faith in the measure and makes it much less likely they will use the information for decision-making. There is also the opportunity for people to use this difference to completely reject what the data is saying, particularly if they don't like the message.

There are a lot of reasons why the situation could arise. Sometimes this comes about because we're actually talking about two different things with a similar-sounding name. Other times there are variations in how the KPI is calculated. Often there are just mistakes or failure to include certain datasets in the KPI calculation. All three of these types of problem can be eased with a KPI definition sheet (see Step 5 for how to set up one of these up).

Checklist

Deal with multiple sets of 'similar' data

❑ Create a KPI definition sheet for each KPI/measure - this makes sure you are talking about precisely the same measure.

❑ Track, record and investigate incidents of contradictory values - this helps you track problems and spot patterns in errors.

❑   If the discrepancy is a symptom of some underlying
      structural issues with the data, be open and honest about
      this and develop a plan for tackling the underlying issues.

Problem 3 - Data existing in different forms

This, for instance, may cover different time spans, different
geographic areas or different business units. This makes it
impossible to consolidate in a meaningful way and can be a
really thorny issue. One of my recent clients had previously
merged with another organisation. Four years after the merger,
the original 'core' firm was still using a 12-month year for its
financials and the 'merged' business was still using a 13-period
(4 weeks per period) financial year. Aggregating and comparing
data was an utter nightmare that required a completely new IT
platform to resolve properly.

Hopefully your issues are not as serious as those in my example.
Solutions to the problem normally fall into one of these
categories:

- An Excel 'fudge' - probably the most common solution.
- 'Data marts' - databases that aggregate existing data
  and have more structure and stability than the Excel
  solution.
- Third party tools for connecting directly to source data
  across multiple sources e.g. SAS Grid.
- A fundamental IT solution - expensive, risky and time-
  consuming.

The first option is the most frequently used. It can work well but
requires real discipline and very good manual systems to keep
it reliable and accurate. Here are some of the things you need to
have in place to keep things on track:

Checklist

Deal with data that exists in different forms

❏   A central document showing where the definitive sources of data are.

❏   A change log for all business-critical spreadsheets.

❏   Locked-down spreadsheets for any sensitive spreadsheets or calculations, with a controlled list of users with write permission.

❏   Detailed process maps showing where data comes from and goes to, kept up to date by named individuals.

❏   A sign-off process for any critical calculations in those spreadsheets.

The more complex an organisation or the more critical the data, the more important these spreadsheet housekeeping disciplines become.

On that last point, here's a great example from the BBC News website in April 2013 of why this is critical:

True Story

It takes an expert to really mess it up

An article by Professor Carment Reinhart and Ken Rogoff (former chief economist for the International Monetary Fund) described how growth slows dramatically when a country's debt rises above 90% of Gross Domestic Product (the overall size of a country's economy).

This paper was widely studied by governments and was used as a major justification for introducing austerity measures.

Thomas Herndon, a student at the University of Massachusetts Amherst, was unable to reproduce the results of the analysis. He wrote to the authors of the paper and asked for the spreadsheet. They sent him the spreadsheet.

'Everyone says seeing is believing, but I almost didn't believe my eyes,' he said.

He had discovered that the Harvard professors had only included 15 of the 20 countries in their analysis for the calculation of average GDP growth in countries with high debt. He also discovered other errors that compounded the problem, and some countries' data was missing completely!

The revised analysis showed a much less stark relationship between national debt and slower growth, with a number of notable exceptions.

This is a quick summary, you can find the original article at **http://www.bbc.co.uk/news/magazine-22223190**

Problem 4 - Lack of trust in the data

Strangely, this is one of the most common ones, leading to the question 'Why on earth are you collecting it?' Start with that exact question. If the need melts away, then just stop collating and reporting that data. If it turns out to be potentially useful and important, then you need to look at repairing trust.

Checklist

Deal with lack of trust in the data

❑ Understand precisely what data is being used, and for what purpose.

❑ Survey the key stakeholders and identify, through structured interviews, which data is of particular concern. (see 'Talk to key stakeholders and subject matter experts' on page 30 for details on how to do this).

❑ Shortlist high-priority data. There's no point in trying to tackle everything at once.

❑ List out the high-priority data and the concerns gathered around that data.

❑ Do a very detailed investigation of a few specific elements of the high-priority data.

❏   If there are no issues identified, broaden the analysis.

❏   If issues are identified, develop a remediation plan and review with your sponsor.

❏   If agreed, implement a remediation action plan.

❏   Put in place controls to ensure that things stay on track.

Problem 5 - Large delays in the collection and collation of the data

Dashboards and reports generally involve dozens, if not hundreds, of pieces of information being gathered together. The final production date of any report or document is going to be determined by the slowest delivery of a piece of information.

So what can you do to mitigate some of these problems? In the order that I'd suggest you try them, here are three options.

Checklist

Deal with delays in the collection of data

❏   Develop a publication timetable, with clear data input deadlines - it is important that this is realistic and has contingency for real-world disruptions.

❏   Process map the reporting 'supply chain' if the input deadlines are not clear or agreed.

❏   Apply SMED method to reduce the cycle time (more on this in a moment).

You can only use SMED if you have already mapped the process, which is why it is the third option listed above.

Speed up data collection using SMED

So what the heck is SMED?

SMED is a great tool with a terrible name. It's this approach that enables McLaren Formula One teams to change a tyre in 2.31 seconds when it takes a normal human being 20 minutes. The tool (actually approach is probably a better description) was developed by Shigeo Shingo. He was consulting with Toyota in the 1950s and 60s and was trying to stop the body shop - an area with huge metal dies for stamping out car body parts - being a bottleneck in the process. Using SMED - or Single Minute Exchange of Dies - they brought the changeover times down from hours (sometimes days) to a few minutes.

SMED is best learnt through hands-on workshops. Here's a quick checklist for the key steps in applying it. I would recommend getting a good book on the method or, even better, signing up for a workshop (Made to Measure KPIs do a tailored in-house session if you need one).

Checklist

Using SMED: Observe the process

❏ Observe the process. (You could video it if it is a user-driven process that takes place in one spot.)

❏ Note down the duration of the major activities. Identify the sequence and dependencies of major activities.

❏ Identify whether activities are internal (must stop the process to do them) or external (can be done without holding up the majority of report production activities).

❏ Draw a Gantt chart showing internal and external operations in different colours/patterns (see example in fig. 7.2 on page 104).

Checklist

Using SMED: Identify internal activities

❑ Which data can you check and validate offline and prior to the report production? How would you do this?

❑ What data and extracts need to be delivered before the process (e.g. report production) can run?

❑ How could this production and supply be streamlined?

❑ What condition does the process need to be in to produce the report? Can people and IT kit be prepared in advance?

❑ What adjustments and changes take place during report production?

❑ Which of them would benefit from function standardisation (e.g. pre-written queries, macros and batch jobs)?

❑ What makes the operator hunt and search for data or commentary during report production? How can you make sure the relevant information is easily to hand, organised efficiently and ready to use?

❑ When do you have to perform complex and fiddly tasks, relying on complex sequences and user memory?

❑ Can you use code, macros or scripts to fully, or partially, automate complex and mistake-prone manipulation? Could manipulation be avoided altogether with a sensible redesign?

❑ Can testing and checking of the reports be improved?

❑ Can you learn from previous mistakes?

❑ What is the most rational testing regime - 100% inspection or statistically based sampling?

Checklist

Using SMED: Remove or reduce internal operations

❑ Once you have identified both internal and external activities, group internal activities together. This will help minimise the time that the process has to be paused.

❑ Convert internal operations to external operations. E.g. Run a query on a spare PC in advance, rather than tying up an analyst's PC during report generation.

❏   Reduce complexity of compulsory internal operation.

Checklist

Using SMED: External Activities

❏   Make sure that external operations really are external, i.e. you don't pause the process to do them.

❏   Reduce time spent on external activities. It won't reduce the setup time in the way that streamlining the internal activities does, but will reduce the total effort required for report production.

Example

Setup time reduction examples

• Reduce the number of source databases or spreadsheets used in report production.

• Reduce the amount of manual spreadsheet manipulation required, possibly through use of macros or improved design.

• Reduce the number of data entry errors through automatic logic checking of fields.

Task	Effort
1) **Regular Account and IAS Forecast**	
1.1) Regular accounts forecast by product	1d 6h
1.2) Regular accounts – create forecast	1h
1.3) Instant Access Savings – Extract inflows, outflows…	2h
1.4) Instant Access Savings. Create forecast	4h
1.5) Review-current accounts–Instant Access–forecasts	2h
1.6) Produce Forecast slides and email for Charlie Crisp…	1h
1.7) Face-to-face with Charlie Crisp	2h
1.8) Send out Forecast	1h
1.9) Sign off Forecast	1h
2) **Assets Forecast**	1h
2.1) Back book modelling	3h
2.2) New business. Meeting with production managers	1h
2.3) Retail mortgage forecast	2h
2.4) New business pipeline analysis	2h
2.5) Back book modelling	1d
2.6) Platform mortgage forecast	3h
2.7) New business back book analysis	1h
2.8) Unsecured, loans, cards, overdrafts	1h
2.9) Review forecasts	0.25h
2.10) Email commentary	0.25h
2.11) Face-to-face with Dominic Dorito	> 0h
2.12) Send out assets forecast	0.25h
3) **Deposit savings**	4d 6h
3.1) Market/competitor data market position	1d
3.2) ISA retention analysis, intention analysis	1d
3.3) Analytics: sales maturities, transfers etc	1d 1h
3.4) Pricing	1d
3.5) Produce DS forecast	4h
3.6) Face-to-face with Freya Fry	1h
3.7) Sign off DS – Freya Fry	
4) Sign off assets – Dominic Dorito	1d
5) Build Pack – Quentin Quaver	6h
6) Pre-meet-week one	1d
7) Submit to Exec Committee Preparatory Meeting	1d
8) ECPM Signoff	1d
9) Monthly forecasting meeting	1d

Dates: 15 Mar, 18 Mar, 19 Mar, 20 Mar, 21 Mar, 22 Mar, 25 Mar

(1.9 effort: > 3d 4.75h)

Fig. 7.2: An example showing internal and external operations on a Gantt chart to help with a cycle time reduction project. Internal operations are the lighter bars, external the darker bars and the critical path is highlighted with a glowing outline.

Recap on applying SMED cycle time reduction to KPI processes

- Understand how the data moves and where it starts and finishes.

- Put together a detailed and practical timetable laying out who needs to do what and when with the data.

- Make sure there are well-defined owners and those owners are prepared to flag up problems and chase the right people when needed.

Resist the temptation to rush into IT solutions

When faced with the five typical problems you may decide to implement an IT system to solve them. If you go ahead and create the IT system without using the techniques recommended here you are likely to fail.

Why? You haven't been through the 'circle of tedium' which is required to get a KPI/measures collection system working properly.

The circle of tedium and why it's useful

The circle of tedium is the slow and painful process of checking where data comes from, finding it's a mess, trying to fix it, finding it is still not working as intended, putting in more fixes etc., etc. From experience, it normally takes **at least 3 to 4 iterations** before the system is working well and everyone has confidence in it. The mistake that many organisations make is that they will do a simple analysis of 'the information we need' and 'the information we have available' and they will jump straight to a system specification. This first pass is invariably flawed in many ways. The problem is if you go straight to a system specification, any mistakes or incorrect assumptions start to be set in computer code and it becomes a lot harder and more expensive to fix.

More Lean methods that can improve KPI production

This is not a book on Lean techniques but I think it is worth mentioning a couple more tools from Lean that are especially useful for improving KPI production.

5S to improve workplace organisation

5S is a workplace organisation philosophy that focuses on visual management and good organisation. There are plenty of books on the approach, though they are mostly focused on manufacturing organisations. It can apply very well to information-based environments.

5S means:

Sorting - Optimise your storage so that documents:
- Are in a logical, self-explanatory network location.
- Do not require interminable levels of navigation through folder hierarchy to access them.
- Are clearly identified with relevant data (like date of issue).
- Make use of good layout, logical structure and correct internal signposting and indexing to ensure information is accessible.

Sweeping or Shine - Eliminate what is not required. This applies not just to the dashboard or report itself but that mess of data and sheets behind the scenes. The clutter in those source spreadsheets is slowing you down and making mistakes more likely.

Straightening or Setting in Order - Clean up databases, removing bad or inconsistent records.

Standardising - Create standard procedures that are highly visual and are a true reflection of the report production process e.g. user-guides and checklists.

Sustaining - Manage skills and training in a systematic way, for example, with visual Skills Matrix wall boards.

Successful 5S will:
- Improve speed of access to data or commentary.
- Reduce 'hunting' time for data and other inputs.
- Highlight shortages during external, not internal, time.

Use a structured method to solve problems
- PDCA cycle for recurrent problems (see page 150).
- P-M analysis for intractable problems (see P-M Analysis by Shirose, Kaneda and Kimura, in the Bibliography).

Do it Again!
To get the best possible 'cycle time' may require several rounds of improvement activity. If you do revisit the same report production process, make sure it's the best use of your time.

Tip

If the worst happens
Even with the best approach in the world, there will still be times when data is not produced. Where it's unavoidable, I would suggest leaving the data out of the final report but still producing the report on time, making it clear where data is missing and why. Holding back a report because of missing information can send out very poor messages to those who have managed to submit their data on time, such as 'the deadline doesn't really matter' or 'their data is not really that important'. With manual systems in particular, getting people into a regular routine or habit is absolutely critical to the success of the system.

Step 7 - Go live - Data problems

Collect data

What are your technology options?

This is a complicated field which could justify several books. It's also an area that moves quite quickly so any in-depth book needs frequent revisions to avoid becoming out of date. However, looking at it at a high level you have a few options for collecting data. For each of these I've outlined very briefly how the given data collection approach would work and what key things should be on your high-level checklist.

The main methods of data collection are:

- Excel
- SharePoint
- Paper documents
- Customised existing system
- ERP/CRM/Workflow data extraction
- Third-party data capture software

Let's look at each of these in turn.

Using Excel for data collection

This is the granddaddy of all data collection systems. It's the one that I see being used most often when something is done quickly and in an ad hoc manner. Let's look at the pros and cons:

Pros

- Often quick to set up.
- Most people in an office environment can use Excel to a basic level.
- Excel exists on most desktops already, avoiding potentially long-winded IT approval processes.
- Can be very flexible.
- Analysis can be quick and easy.
- Easy to import and export data to other applications.

- Can be integrated with SharePoint for additional robustness.

Cons

- Mixes source data with analysis, which is convenient but ultimately risky.
- Can become unstable with multiple linked spreadsheets.
- Complexity piles up rapidly.
- Although Excel supports field-locking and collaborative working it can be unstable and a bit scary, particularly in earlier versions such as 2003.
- Many solutions I've seen are not maintained or backed-up properly.
- Requires careful locking-down of formulas and layout to prevent end-user changes to data input sheets.
- Rapidly becomes unwieldy with very large datasets.

Using SharePoint for data collection

SharePoint has rapidly grown into a fairly sophisticated collaborative working environment. It is used in lots of businesses I know, but generally it is an obsolete version. This means I probably have a slightly jaded view of its capabilities and flexibility.

Pros

- There's a proper database behind the scenes to keep things organised.
- You can set up Excel spreadsheets in SharePoint so that SharePoint takes care of multiple simultaneous edits.
- Surveys and forms are pretty easy to create.

Cons

- You need some technical support to set up a SharePoint site.
- There is inevitably some 'borrowing' of existing sites required to get small projects up and running - in my clients it has been a constant struggle.

- In pre 2010 versions of SharePoint (i.e. the versions still used in many organisations) customising forms is complex/impossible.

So SharePoint trades some of the flexibility of Excel for improved data integrity and robustness. It's a good solution where you need an Excel-like interface shared across a work group, or quick and easily collection of survey data. Where it seems to be lacking is in the rapid collection of small chunks of data throughout the day. In this situation the user interface makes it a painful experience to collect data.

Paper documents - manual data capture

It may surprise you to see this antique technology on the list but there are still some things you can do with paper sheets which are just not possible with any other system.

Pros

- Very quick to deploy.
- Everybody knows how to fill it in.
- Does not take up computer desktop space.
- Allows additional comments without restriction.
- Shows that a human being will be looking at this data.
- Visible and hard to ignore.

Cons

- Will require re-keying of data.
- Requires physical collection of sheets.
- Changing the form requires a new print run and can require version control.
- Forms can run out.

Of all the options here I would never recommend running a paper data collection system in the medium or long term. Paper systems are very good for creating very short-term prototypes and gathering small sets of data very quickly.

Key features of effective manual data collection systems:

- A proper definition of what is measured by whom and when.
- A decent collection timetable. By decent I mean there is enough time to visit the person collecting the data, sort out any problems, format it and forward to those people who need it.
- Visibility of when there are problems. This would include a 'problems log' which is reviewed by the management team and clearly defined owners who are collecting the right data in line with the collection timetable.

Tip

There is a long term trend to move towards IT systems for obvious reasons, but one of the unsung benefits of a manual data collection system is that extra information gets passed down the chain and obviously erroneous information can be queried early on as it goes through human brains rather than just an IT system.

The other less obvious benefit of the manual system is that people are lazy. And I don't mean this in a bad way, but there is a real reluctance in people to collect and collate information that they know isn't used or is in some way flawed. A risk with a heavily-automated system is that you can create an ocean of useless and unread reports at the click of a button.

Data collection - Customised existing system

This is a really broad category. The conversation normally goes along the lines of 'We have customer service system X, why can't we just add a little dialogue box to capture Y and a button to capture data item Z?'

Pros

- Avoids the need for additional systems documents.
- Keeps the consistent user interface which people are familiar with.
- Potentially allows the collection of useful system-generated data automatically and simultaneously with user-entered data.

Cons

- Has all the associated risks that come with software development, i.e. budget creep, scope creep and risk of project failure.
- Requires very clear project specification at the start (when, in my experience, people often aren't actually that clear on what they need or want).
- Can introduce operational risk if these additions are to a production environment.
- Typically implementation can be a very slow and expensive option.
- Normally involves external IT vendor support or specialist contractor resource.
- Often encounters massive opposition from the internal IT functions.

If this option has a place, it's normally the last mile of a long KPI journey, where you are perhaps replacing an existing clunky data collection system with something more permanent. It is important to know what you are getting into and that you have the internal IT and project management skills to land it successfully. If there is **any doubt** about a successful outcome I would strongly advise **not** going down this route.

ERP / CRM / Workflow data extraction

Most organisations these days have large systems in the background collecting data about their operation. If you are lucky enough to already be collecting most of the information you need, then setting up automated data extraction from the systems is a tempting option. Many of the risks and benefits are similar to those for the previous section. The main difference is that this approach will eliminate some of the operational and development risk.

Pros

- Potentially invisible to the end-user - making it the ideal solution if all the data you need is already collected.
- Can be fully automated.
- Will already be tested and validated.
- Does not require new IT systems software.

Cons

- Becomes very problematic if you need to supplement existing data collection with user comments - this requires development of a new user interface and all the development risk and cost that goes with it.

- In many systems access to the production database is restricted or protected, requiring a mirror database to be set up for the data analytics. This can be complex and expensive.

- In a fully automated system much of the data is not scrutinised by real human beings. It becomes easy to miss crucial gaps and mistakes in the data that may ultimately undermine the quality of the analyses being performed.

Although this may look like a very appealing option, my experience is that it never works out quite as elegantly, cheaply or speedily as you anticipate. Like the 'customised existing system' option, this is one for a more mature organisation that is absolutely clear it has the data that is required and knows what it is getting into from a systems perspective.

Third-party data capture systems

There is a class of software called 'desktop analytics', or as one of my clients put it, 'spycam'.

The way the software works is to hook into the Windows API (Application Programming Interface - the method by which programs interact with the operating system).

This approach enables a small program on the user's desktop to identify what is happening on the desktop and to flag that certain activities are happening when key trigger events are detected. This seems to work well in environments with well-defined processes that are predominantly PC-based. Three vendors are currently prominent in this space, OpenSpan, Verint (Impact 360) and Nice (RTAM). These systems will normally allow you to add metadata (supplemental data) through the use of drop-down customisable menus or text boxes. Once up and running, the system can be a very valuable way to gather problem-related data, metadata and user comments.

Pros

- Can be tuned to gather just the information you need to know.
- Based on a robust database back-end, for example, SQL or Cognos.
- Less complex than developing a system from scratch.

Cons

- Will require configuration which can be extensive if you have poorly defined processes.
- Requires ongoing external vendor's support contract.
- Not as flexible as other (less permanent) solutions such as Excel.
- Requires budget, support and IT engagement.

116

So, to summarise, the three options you are most likely to be using on a regular basis, in the short to medium term, are Excel, SharePoint and paper capture sheets. The other options outlined here are technically more elegant and are likely to be more robust but also become projects in their own right and need to be treated with caution if they are on the 'critical path' for your KPI implementation.

Here is a selection checklist that should help you identify which of these options is best for you:

Checklist

Data capture method selection

- ❏ How permanent does the solution need to be?
- ❏ Are you prepared to find funding and set up a project for new software?
- ❏ How many users will be involved in collecting data?
- ❏ Is your IT department engaged and supportive?
- ❏ How big does the dataset need to be?
- ❏ What kind of analysis will be done on the data?
- ❏ Is free text involved?
- ❏ What expansion plans are likely to be involved? This will affect the nature of data collected and the architecture you choose.

There's an awful lot to take on board when you're collecting data. It's easy to miss some of the critical points, so here's a checklist that can help you make sure you have nailed most or all of the important aspects of collecting data.

Checklist

Data collection

❏ Is the source of data defined by role? It's important to make sure that you don't just have someone's name as a data source, but that the data is assigned to a role. If a person is ill or moves on you still know where the data comes from. It's also important to have this as part of someone's role so there is a formal recognition that it will take up some of that individual's time each period.

❏ Is the data collection a reasonable task? How long does it take to collect information and check it, is it reasonable and does the person tasked with gathering it agree to commit that much time to the task?

❏ Is there a check in place to ensure that the data is collected and submitted in a timely way? Is there a system to follow-up missing or incorrect data?

❏ Do you have a KPI definition for the data you are collecting (see the section, 'Define your KPIs' on page 62)?

❏ Does the person providing the data understand precisely what is required of them and when?

❏ Is there a contingency plan for providing the data in the event of sickness or holiday?

❏ Do you have a backup plan for the historic KPI data? Many organisations I have worked with delete or overwrite data and subsequently regret it.

❏ Does the data collection have a very senior sponsor? Without some kind of management sponsorship, data collection will rapidly fall to one side.

Analyse data

Find the right analysis tool in a fast-moving field

For many people, this is the fun part. Fortunately, the market is extremely well served with data analysis and data exploration tools. This is a fast-moving market with multiple major players. My first port of call when I'm looking at analytical tools for clients is to look at the Gartner BI Magic Quadrant report (BI stands for 'Business Intelligence'). The whole point of the Gartner report is to help you understand which are the best offerings. The reports are generally balanced, insightful and well worth the effort.

As this report reflects very well on the top-ranked vendors, you will normally find that one of them gives away the Gartner report free of charge (as of 2013 it is Tableau). It's a thorough document, taking two or three hours to digest properly, but in it you will discover which are the top-ranked tools for your particular needs.

Each tool has a 'sweet spot' - the purpose for which it was specifically developed. Although many of the tools, and in particular the big players, will claim to do everything, you will find with experience that they are better at some things than others.

Here are some of the questions you should be asking yourself when you're choosing which analytical tools to use:

Checklist

Choose the right analysis tool

❏   What analytical tools do you use currently in your organisation?

❏   What is your organisation's current IT policy on preferred analytical tool solutions?

❏   Do you have any tools for which you are licensed but aren't currently using those licences?

❏   What is your budget?

- ❏ What analytical and software skills exist within your team?
- ❏ Is your organisation comfortable with 'software as a service' (SAS)?
- ❏ Will the tool host the data in its own database or will it 'suck the data' from existing data sources?
- ❏ What legacy systems would any analytical tools have to interface with?
- ❏ What type of output are you looking for? E.g. static paper reports, live web-served analysis, self-service etc.

Tip

When to be pragmatic with analytical tools

Having worked extensively in financial services organisations, I bear the scars of very slow and conservative IT policies. I've learnt through tough experience that it is often quicker to be pragmatic and use an existing, although sub-optimal, tool than to fight the fight for the 'ideal tool'.

Like most people, I have some certain 'old favourites' that I like to use. Two of these fall into the 'data exploration' category. These tools are TIBCO Spotfire and Tableau. Both tools have a similar sweet spot which is rapid, very intuitive exploration of existing data from multiple sources. As a bonus, both applications have outstanding presentational standards, showing many of the characteristics that I urge my clients to aspire to - simplicity, restraint and visual clarity.

The analytical tool that you will most likely end up using is Excel, maybe fed with some output from an SQL database or an Oracle query. There's nothing wrong with this as such, but it may be worth aiming a bit higher in the medium to long term.

Frequency of measuring and reporting - Finding the KPI 'heartbeat'

It may sound like an obvious question, but have you asked yourself 'How often do you need to measure this?' If you measure things

121

too often you risk drowning in unnecessary work and seeing little benefit. At the other extreme, not measuring often enough means that decision-making can be delayed and some or all of the benefits of the measurement will evaporate.

The most common reasons for choosing a reporting frequency are 'That's how often the report is generated at the moment' and everything is driven 'by the accounting cycle' (even if it's non-financial data). These really are not good enough reasons in themselves, although of course the optimal frequency may have been chosen purely by chance.

There is no golden rule here, but the next checklist raises some points that should help steer you to a sensible reporting frequency:

Checklist

Decide on reporting frequency

❏ How long does it take to collect the data?

❏ What effort is required to collect the data? (Try adding it up in 'person days'.)

❏ What is the longest period over which you will typically get little meaningful change?

❏ After what period of time does the data become meaningless or less relevant?

❏ How long does it take to implement actions based on the data? The point here is that this is part of your information-to-reaction-time.

❏ What is the shortest interval, after an incident, that things can go seriously wrong without detection? (See also the FMEA approach on page 126.) Your reporting frequency needs to catch an issue **before** it becomes a crisis.

So, data which changes very rapidly and is very easy to collect would be a candidate for a high sampling-rate. Examples of this might include stock prices, airplane altitude or number of customers on hold in a call centre.

Situations where you would have a much longer sampling interval might include customer satisfaction scores, inflation rates or staff turnover figures.

True Story

Random results generator!

I've seen a number of examples at either end of the scale. With one client, involved in a complex chemical process, we discovered that the process frequently varied outside of its control limits within 10 to 15 minutes, but they were sampling once every **24 hours**. At the other end of the scale I have seen call centres obsessively tracking 'average handling times', when in reality the variation they were seeing was purely statistical scatter. The call centre situation is a good example of 'We have the information easily accessible, so we're going to use it.'

The ideal sampling interval often won't be the same as the actual sampling interval. Before you get too perfectionist, the best approach is to use what you currently have but also make sure you have recorded what your ideal is, so you have some improvement aims visible. Make sure that you think about and record your 'ideal sampling frequency' in your KPI definitions database (see page 63).

Start small - Running a 'proof of concept'

Situations vary but it is best to start with a small pilot implementation if at all possible. Sometimes there are situations where this is not possible, for example where there is intense pressure from the industry regulator. Be warned though, skipping straight to a full roll-out will increase the practical risk involved in your system implementation.

Checklist

Run a 'proof of concept' for the new system

❏ Identify the number of users you need for the proof of concept to be meaningful.

❏ Identify the functionally different day-to-day operations you need to include for the results to be meaningful.

❏ Include variations in the IT landscape, for example, different legacy IT systems in use.

❏ Assess the consequences of partial or complete proof of concept failure - is there an operational or service risk?

❏ Gain commitment from senior management that if the proof of concept is successful it will be expanded.

❏ Document success criteria.

❏ Create proof of concept project charter.

❏ Review proof of concept against success criteria.

IT project memory jogger

The usual high-level questions you need to consider for any IT project are included in the checklist below.

Checklist

IT project memory jogger

- ❏ How and where will the data and software be physically hosted?
- ❏ What are the data security/data protection considerations?
- ❏ Who are the stakeholders in the IT project?
- ❏ What are the associated business-as-usual costs? For example, hosting, maintenance contracts and internal support costs.
- ❏ Are there any regulator specific requirements?
- ❏ Is the software you're looking at on the preferred vendor list?
- ❏ What is the approval process for new software?
- ❏ Are there any other network/infrastructure considerations?
- ❏ Are there any privacy laws that you need to consider (especially true of mainland Europe and particularly Switzerland)?
- ❏ What full-time project resource/support is required?
- ❏ Who is paying the bill?
- ❏ What other internal approval processes do you need to comply with?

Manage risk using FMEA

One of the tools most commonly used to measure and manage risk is called FMEA or Failure Mode and Effects Analysis.

Whilst the name is about as user-friendly as a barbed-wire apple, the underlying concept is both useful and powerful. Here is a very quick guide to FMEA. There are plenty of other books that will give you background detail.

FMEA is an approach developed to allow you to compare and balance problems that are unlikely but very serious with others that may be more frequent but much less serious. It gives you a way of balancing risk and probability in a numeric way. This can help you balance the terrifying but unusual (catastrophic plane crash) with the minor but frequent (hitting thumb with a hammer).

Checklist

Manage risk with FMEA

❏ Go through your system or process and ask the question 'What happens if this fails?'.

❏ Document the consequential events from a system failure.

❏ Assign a score for probability, using a 1 to 10 scale.

❏ Assign a score for severity of the consequence using a 1 to 10 scale.

❏ Calculate the probability multiplied by the severity.

❏ Use this total score to identify **high-scoring** risks and prioritise these for mitigating actions.

Example

Falling asleep when driving FMEA

Failure: Falling asleep whilst driving

Failure mode: Late night driving, lack of rest or breaks

Consequence: Potential total loss of life for those in the car and/or others

The probability of this happening = **2**
The severity of this failure = **10**
Total score = **20**

Poor visibility when driving FMEA

Failure: Crash due to poor visibility

Failure mode: User forgets to check and refill wash-wipe before journey

Consequence: Potential total loss of life for those in the car

The probability of this happening = **8**
The severity of this failure = **10**
Total score = **80**

Calibrate your FMEA scores

You probably spotted the weak point in this approach, which is the subjectivity of the 1 to 10 scoring scale. It is a subjective judgement. You can greatly improve the robustness and credibility of your analysis by creating a calibrated scale. You would do this typically by giving specific relevant examples of what would score 1, 5 and 10. This enables the person completing the FMEA to reference back to the calibrated scale.

Once you have identified high-scoring risks and issues the next step is to 'head them off at the pass'. You do this by creating 'mitigations' or things that you would do differently to avoid the problem and then re-score using the same process to show the new improved score.

So, in practice, to use this you would create a spreadsheet with the following headings:

- Failure description (what happens)
- Mode description (how it happens)
- Consequence/Effect
- Probability - score out of 10
- Severity - score out of 10
- FMEA Score (severity x probability)
- Mitigation
- Revised probability
- Revised severity
- Revised FMEA Score

Here's an extract from a simple FMEA sheet:

Failure	Mode	Effect	Probability	Severity	Score	Mitigation
Missing data	Data sheets not completed	Missing or incomplete data	9	7	**63**	Implement tracking log
Missing data	Complete data sheets not returned	Missing or incomplete data	6	7	**42**	Document process and have backup 'collectors'
Missing data	Run out of capture sheets	Missing or incomplete data	8	9 (affects all team)	**72**	Put in sheet 'kanban' - restock on low levels
Missing data	Staff not aware of requirement	Missing or incomplete data	8	5 (only new or temp staff affected)	**40**	Add to induction training

Fig. 7.3: An example FMEA matrix

To the right of the 'Mitigation' column it is sensible to add more scoring columns to show the score that you should expect once the mitigation actions have been put in place. You may also add some action-tracking fields to keep the implementation of the mitigations on track. To keep things readable, I've not included these columns in the example above.

Tip

Detectability and FMEA

You can also refine this matrix by adding an additional column called Detection. For instance, it is often hard to know when you are about to fall asleep so this would have a high score for Detection, whereas a windscreen with lots of grot is easy to spot, making it unlikely you would let it get to a dangerous level - a high score implies low detectability, bumping up your score.

If you use a detectability value, your FMEA score becomes probability x severity x detectability.

A free FMEA Excel template is available to download from: **http://wp.me/p1H6XP-zD**

Issue a first production version of your report

At some point you will be ready to issue your first KPI report or dashboard. This is a nerve-wracking and quite delicate stage in the process. If you position the first output in the wrong way, or it has obvious fundamental flaws, credibility can be lost and it can be extremely difficult to recover the situation.

Here are some preflight checks you might want to do before you issue KPIs.

Checklist

Preflight check before launching new reports/dashboards

❏ Introduce a 'source sign-off' process so that you have confidence that data sourced from elsewhere is acceptable and endorsed by those providing it.

❏ Publish KPI definitions with the report for reference.

❏ Publish any known issues with the definitions or data within the report and what actions, if any, are being taken to address those issues.

❏ Test the data on a small friendly audience first to help flush out any obvious issues.

❏ Add any caveats to the initial report and explain what issues may be expected on the first pass.

❏ Sit down with key stakeholders and walk them through the report before they are presented with it in any public forum so that they feel comfortable with the contents and can privately express any concerns or ask any questions.

❏ If you key stakeholders are comfortable, make sure they explicitly confirm this to you.

Tip

Keep the team up to date on report improvements

You may choose to include a report development update with each issue to show what has changed from previous issues and any problems that you have identified or tackled. Make sure you make it easy for people to contact you or the report's author with feedback. Add names and contact details to every document that you produce.

Put your KPIs into production and document the process

Your first pass on gathering data and doing the analysis will normally be a bit of a muddled process. Once you have been round the cycle a few times you will start to have a better-defined process which you then need to formalise so it becomes reliable and reproducible.

Documentation is a really important part of putting KPIs into production. You need to be able to clearly show and explain the process to those involved and to compare what's really happening with what should be happening once you're up and running. The tool for this is process mapping.

Map KPI production

Why is process mapping in a book on KPIs?

Process mapping is a really familiar tool to many people. It is used in just about every improvement methodology. I almost hesitate to talk about it in this book because it is so commonly used. But interestingly I don't see it used very often for KPI production so I have included a short section showing the basics of how to create a simple process map for your KPI production process.

Mapping your KPI production can have a number of benefits:

- Provides a complete end-to-end overview of the KPI production process (often for the first time).
- Engages the process owners in dialogue, with them clearly in the 'expert' position - very good for buy-in.
- Enables process improvement and simplification work.
- Creates the foundation for lead-time reduction work, skills management and audits.

Process mapping conventions

There are really three basic symbols that you need to get started with process mapping:

Fig. 7.4: The most common process mapping symbols

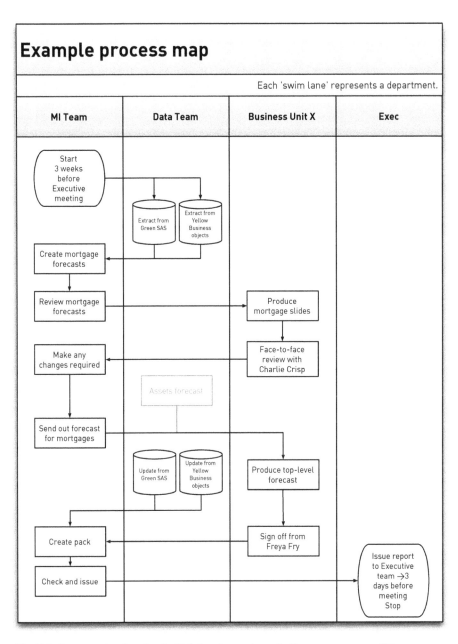

Fig. 7.5: An example of a simple high-level report production process map. This one uses swim lanes to show ownership of each step.

Trap

Process mapping levels - why they are important and tricky

One of the trickiest things about process mapping is coming to terms with the concept of 'levels' and then defining them in a consistent and repeatable way.

The best way to show this difference is to use a simple example such as using the bathroom in the morning.

- At a high level you could have a process step box called 'use the bathroom'.
- At a more detailed level you could show 'have a shower', 'clean teeth', 'wash face' etc.
- Going down another level of detail 'clean teeth' can be broken into a number of sub-steps including squeezing toothpaste onto the toothbrush, cleaning specific parts of the mouth and rinsing the toothbrush.

This example shows three different levels of detail on the same process. Why is it important to separate the process into multiple levels? Well, if you run a workshop you will very quickly understand that it becomes impossible to map the process if you go into too much detail too early. Dividing the process into levels helps keep things manageable in terms of process creation and also the physical process mapping.

I'm afraid there is no universal convention on levels, so the best advice I can offer is to create some specific examples that will work across your organisation to illustrate each of the levels and appoint one final arbiter who ensures consistency of approach across all process maps.

Checklist

Build maps of your KPI production process

The process mapping checklist

❏ Decide which tool you're going to use to document your maps (e.g. Visio, PowerPoint, Aris etc.).

❏ Train or requisition process mapping resource if it's a big job.

❏ Find an online or physical repository for your process maps which users can access.

❏ Agree conventions for process mapping.

❏ Create a version control system and revision numbering system.

❏ Agree footer content for process maps.

❏ Decide on contact details for process maps - phone numbers are best, then email.

❏ Identify stakeholders in the process mapping exercise using RACI matrix (see page 28 for more on RACI).

Stakeholders may include:

- Operations
- Risk
- Regulatory
- Data security
- Privacy
- Quality

Checklist

Engage stakeholders in creation and review of process maps

❑ Establish who needs to sign off or approve the KPI process.

❑ Gain sign-off or approval for new KPI process(es).

❑ Put in place a regular review and audit process for new processes.

Actively seek user feedback and tweaks

Most people have dealt with a wide variety of shops. You know from experience that, in some shops, when you take something back with a problem or because you don't like it they will respond cheerfully and helpfully and quickly sort out the refund or replacement. There are other shops where the body language, tone and manner are distinctly prickly - they may even challenge your reason or right to return something. If you deal with the second kind of shop you rapidly become reluctant to have any kind of interaction with them. You know that whatever they say on a mission statement about their returns policy, it is just not very pleasant dealing with them.

It is just the same when you're developing a new KPI process (or any process for that matter). It's really critical to take enormous care not to create an environment that rejects constructive feedback and the reporting of problems. It only takes a couple of offhand comments or someone over enthusiastically explaining why the person giving feedback is wrong, to create a climate that no longer 'welcomes the problem' but rather tries to sweep it under the carpet.

Because much of what is required to create a good feedback environment is intangible, it is hard to create a comprehensive checklist but here are a few things that you should make sure are in place:

Checklist

Gather effective feedback from users

❏ Make sure there is a clear way for stakeholders to give feedback easily and painlessly.

❏ Ensure that giving feedback does not become a 'career-limiting move' for those doing so.

❏ Let people know that positive meaningful action is taking place as a result of feedback.

❏ Don't argue or counter when people are giving feedback.

That last point in particular may be a bit controversial. There are two things going on when someone gives feedback. The first is a reflection of genuine issues with the process that they are telling you about. The second is they are giving you their perception. So even if they are factually wrong, don't trust, or don't understand it properly, then you have a problem - just as much as if the underlying hardware or software is not performing as designed. It is important to think carefully about how to try and fix this perception rather than simply 'arguing back' and risking shutting the door on feedback forever.

Revise and refine your system throughout the 'warranty period'

Rather than leave problems to fester, make changes as quickly as is feasibly possible. The only situation in which you might want to hesitate before doing this is if you make changes to the underlying data schema and risk devaluing the entire process. With this exception in mind, the general motto of early, rigorous, vigorous and enthusiastic improvement is a good one.

Agree a Service Level Agreement

Service Level Agreements (SLAs) are documents used between suppliers and customers to ensure the service meets an agreed level.

SLAs provide a framework against which you can review real-world performance.

I have to be honest: most Service Level Agreements I've seen in real life make my eyes glaze over with boredom. They are normally incredibly long and tedious documents that are effectively tools to beat up third-party suppliers. Whilst on my soapbox, let's look at a few of the issues that I see with the kind of SLAs I'm moaning about:

- They are written for legal recourse not readability. They become highly technical documents that attempt to cover every possible infringement.
- They are written by people who don't really understand the process. The way in which process performance is measured and the elements of a process that are measured show that the individual creating the agreement really doesn't 'get' what is going on.
- Arbitrary service levels are assigned but there is just not enough knowledge about what is reasonable or practical. Often, when challenged why particular figures have been used in the SLA, you rapidly discover that they had been plucked out of thin air.
- Service levels that have never been achieved are set as the official 'standard' even though they are being breached each and every day. Again I've often seen service levels that both parties **know** are unachievable and have never been achieved, and yet they become embodied in the document.

With this still fresh in your mind, let's look at some checklist points that should help you avoid these pitfalls:

Checklist

Set Service Level Agreements

❏ If the SLA document is required to be a legal document, has an abbreviated 'everyday summary' been produced for those running the process?

❏ Have the SLAs been signed off by key stakeholders who run the process?

❏ Has the justification and rationale behind the agreed SLAs been documented?

❏ Have the agreed SLAs been consistently and meaningfully achieved previously?

Step 7 - Go live - Map KPI production

Deal with problems

Common reporting problems

Unresolved problems kill KPIs and reports

Once your system is up and running, you are a long way from being able to leave it. To do so at this stage is likely to be fatal. Problems will spring up that you were not expecting. Sometimes they were always there, sometimes they are introduced. Management control systems are not static things. People are constantly tinkering with them (and rightly so), so there are always new problems being introduced.

Here are some of the most common ones that I see in the workplace:

- Late delivery
- Embarrassing content
- Discredited content
- Excessive effort
- Major unexpected operational crises
- Poor readability
- Long, complex or jargon-littered reports

Let's have a quick look the issues and how you deal with them.

Checklist

Handle late delivery of output

This is one of the most common issues I see with reports. Not only does it leave key decision-makers without information they need to make informed decisions, it also undermines confidence in the management information production process.

When delivery is late:

❏ Are the reasons for the late delivery investigated and reported back to the internal customer as soon as possible?

❏ Can you take corrective action to avoid the delay in future?

❏ If the issues are repeated, are they highlighting an underlying process weakness which you need to address?

❏ Is there an appropriate forum to examine report production performance, and is it reviewed in that forum?

If there seems to be a systemic issue, think about using the cycle time reduction techniques (see page 101.)

Manage embarrassing content

Are you asking a fox to guard the henhouse? Are you asking someone to incriminate themselves with data? It takes a strong individual to sign up to that. It may be worth reallocating responsibility for that particular part of the report to someone with less invested in the output.

Trap

Omission of guilt

The most common form of 'embarrassment censorship' I've seen is omission. A chart or table simply disappears. In a rapidly changing reporting environment it is often the hardest form of censorship to spot. This is why it is important to create, and formally sign off, a definitive report structure. You also need to put in governance requiring formal sign-off before changes can be made.

Checklist

Deal with discredited content

This is definitely a situation in which prevention is better than cure. If you end up in the unfortunate situation where a major issue with the quality of data or reporting has been discovered, here are the things you need to do to ensure that you recover the situation:

❏ Do not 'blagg' or 'bluff' your way through explaining what the issue may or may not be.

❏ Investigate thoroughly the reasons behind the problem.

❏ Be as honest as possible when reporting back.

❏ Ensure that any explanation is clear, contains the remedial actions required and has a credible plan.

The only thing worse than content that has been discredited once is content that has been discredited twice. If you are fortunate enough to get the chance to put it right, make sure you do it properly the second time. Allow enough time, resource and support to fix it properly. Make sure you test any solution very thoroughly before it gets to your internal customer.

Excessive production effort

If it's massively tedious or effort-intensive to create a measure or report, it will often die as soon as that particular burning need has passed. To avoid this, you need to pre-empt any complaint and start to think about semi (or complete) automation wherever possible.

Checklist

Reduce production effort

❏ Have you mapped the process?

❏ Are there redundant steps in the process?

❏ Are there other steps that can be combined?

❏ Is there excessive manual activity, such as copy and paste in Excel, that can be automated or designed out?

❏ Has the process been examined to see whether any redundant or excessive information is being collected and analysed? If so, can it be eliminated?

❏ Are there any other options to simplify the process?

❏ Does the resource have the appropriate seniority for the task involved? For instance, tying up middle managers with tasks that are essentially admin work.

Major unexpected operational crises

Major issues such as product recalls, mergers and natural disasters can wreak havoc with any 'discretionary' activities within an organisation. In one of my clients, senior management stopped having steering meetings for one of the major brands (that represented 25% of their accounts) during a difficult and torrid merger. Unsurprisingly, that particular product went into an almost instantaneous coma the moment those meetings stopped. Four years later, they had still not resumed those steering meetings!

If reporting KPIs is put 'on ice' because of exceptional events, you need to make sure:

❏ The reason for it being put 'on ice' is clearly articulated.

❏ There is intent to revive that measure/report at a future date.

❏ That future date is agreed.

❏ There is a forum for raising any breach of this commitment with stakeholders at the appropriate level.

Checklist

Report readability

It is important to present your report or dashboard clearly. Consider whether **you** would be happy to read it. Some things to consider are:

- ❏ No font size below 8 point. Commentary and body text at a minimum of 10 point. And take note - I have had some senior clients who are partially-sighted, so flex to the situation.
- ❏ No red to green differentiation (this causes difficulties for those with red-green colour blindness, e.g. traffic light indicators).
- ❏ No strongly-coloured text on strongly-coloured background.
- ❏ No overlapping data sets on charts.
- ❏ No double Y axis charts.
- ❏ No mixed chart types (e.g. bar with line).

For a full method for improving readability refer back to 'Review existing reports and dashboards - The Brilliant Dashboards Checklist' on page 78.

Checklist

Report length, complexity and jargon

There is no single golden rule here, but these questions should help decide the appropriateness of the data you're providing:

- ❏ How long would it take to read your complete document properly?
- ❏ How much of the data is there 'just in case'?
- ❏ What justification do you have for the just-in-case data?
- ❏ Are jargon terms and acronyms defined anywhere in the document?
- ❏ Could an intelligent but non-specialist reader make sense of the report without additional input?

If there is a lot of just-in-case data, this can be a symptom of a report that services a poorly focused meeting. It may be worth reviewing whether there is a clear Terms of Reference for the meeting. See 'The basics for a meeting's Terms of Reference' on page 69 for how to do this.

Tip

Use your eyes to find out what people really think about their new reports

One of the most interesting exercises is to watch how your target audience use their new reports in meetings (or whatever the target event is for their use). You should gain access to the relevant meeting, position yourself so you can easily observe what is happening but don't let people know what you are observing.

Questions to ask yourself are:

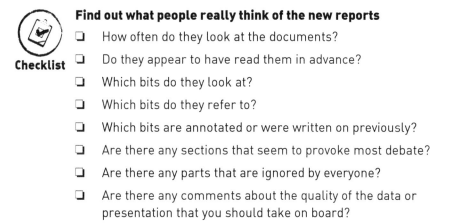

Checklist

Find out what people really think of the new reports

❏   How often do they look at the documents?

❏   Do they appear to have read them in advance?

❏   Which bits do they look at?

❏   Which bits do they refer to?

❏   Which bits are annotated or were written on previously?

❏   Are there any sections that seem to provoke most debate?

❏   Are there any parts that are ignored by everyone?

❏   Are there any comments about the quality of the data or presentation that you should take on board?

Key Idea

KPIs and the improvement cycle

One of my favourite and most overused phrases is 'You don't fatten a pig by weighing it.' It is good to remember that however important KPIs seem, they are only one part of the management process. They fit in as part of what is called the improvement cycle.

One version of the improvement cycle you will almost certainly come across is PDCA, as described by Dr. W. Edwards Deming. This stands for 'plan', 'do', 'check' and 'act'. This version of the improvement cycle is more aimed towards problem-solving as opposed to 'business as usual'.

KPIs are very much in the 'check' step of the improvement cycle.

The key thing about any kind of improvement cycle is that the overall effectiveness of the cycle is limited by the weakest element in that cycle. It doesn't matter if you have perfect KPIs; if you don't act on them they are worthless. Setting up an effective management control system is another book in its own right but here are some checks that should help you identify if you have any problems:

Improvement cycle step 1 - Plan

Lay out the expectations, objectives and steps necessary to achieve the targets or goals.

Checklist

PDCA Plan

❏ There is a clear strategy or set of strategic objectives you are working towards.

❏ You can clearly explain what success looks like.

❏ The stakeholders have been clearly identified and documented, ideally using something like a RACI matrix.

❏ Stakeholders are aware that they are stakeholders.

- ❏ On a day-to-day level, you are clear what you are trying to achieve.
- ❏ There is a timescale associated with what you are trying to achieve.
- ❏ Clear ownership has been assigned to objectives.
- ❏ Correct resources have been allocated to achieve objectives.
- ❏ You have documented what you are trying to achieve.
- ❏ Baseline KPIs measures have:
  - Measure definition
  - Frequency
  - Owner

Improvement cycle step 2 - Do

Deliver on the plan or execute the process to create a product or service. Gather data along the way that feeds the 'check' and 'act' steps of this loop.

PDCA Do

Checklist

- ❏ Make sure an execution plan for the project is in place.
- ❏ Use and review the project plan on a regular basis.
- ❏ Check that the required resources are available and budgeted.
- ❏ Make sure the appropriate tools are available to achieve the task.
- ❏ Make sure that any planned stakeholder time is made available as agreed.
- ❏ Ensure that delivery team(s) are actually meeting with each other at the required frequency.
- ❏ Check that actions are being recorded and managed through an action log.

Improvement cycle step 3 - Check

Analyse the actual results compared with the objectives in the 'plan' step. You are looking for shortfalls or problems here. This step typically involves formal analysis of the data.

Checklist

PDCA Check

❏ Are there at least 10 to 30 representative data points recorded for measurement?

❏ Is the data summarised in a meaningful way?

❏ Is the data presented with all the required features and information but no additional visual clutter?

❏ Are data tables required and present?

❏ Has appropriate, relevant and rational commentary been added?

❏ Has the analysis been shared with the key stakeholders identified in the 'plan' step?

❏ Is the output of the analysis shared in good time to allow stakeholders to prepare for reviews, ask questions and form sensible judgements?

❏ Are the **mechanisms** by which real-world events are driving the KPI understood?

If the answer to that last question is 'no' then it may be time to employ a structured problem-solving tool such as P-M analysis. See the entry for 'P-M Analysis' by Shirose, Kaneda and Kimura in the Bibliography for more on this.

Improvement cycle step 4 - Act

This step is about putting things right to bring the real-world activity back on track or in line with the goals stated in the Plan step.

Checklist

PDCA Act

❏ Are all stakeholders in agreement on the importance of action?

❏ Has dissent and disagreement been discussed and resolved?

❏ Are adequate resources in place to act?

❏ Has necessary process downtime been agreed with process owners?

❏ Are resources available for fixing the issues?

❏ Is budget available (if required)?

❏ Have notes on changes and fixes been made and shared for future reference?

Tip

The secret to making the improvement cycle work well

Improvement cycles are never a single-pass loop. They need multiple passes before they start working properly. Awareness of the way in which the steps join together helps you develop a process 'conscience' - an awareness that enables you to spot problems with the loop and fix them. It's a case of applying PDCA to itself.

Hand over to 'business as usual' team

Assuming that you are not the management information team, business intelligence team or reporting team within your organisation then you will probably need to do some kind of handover once the KPIs have been set up and are running properly. If you followed the earlier checklists you should have most of what you need already prepared. Here's a final checklist to make sure you have the important things covered:

Checklist

Handover to 'business as usual' teams

❏ Full definition of each KPI - documented on paper and/or in a database.

❏ Process map(s) showing the production process for each measure or KPI.

❏ User guides for the individuals producing each measure or KPI.

❏ A sensible SLA document, written for human beings, covering agreed service levels with the rationale behind those levels. If this document is complex, then you will need a summary document for quick and easy reference.

❏ Templates, spreadsheets etc. for producing output reports and dashboards.

❏ An action log showing what has happened and anything that is still outstanding.

❏ Make sure that every action has a 'who', 'when', 'how' and 'what' associated with it.

❏ A list, with contact details, of each key person involved in the production of these documents.

❏ Book a follow-up session to make sure the handover has gone smoothly.

Sustain your new KPIs

If you have made it through the entire KPI development journey and are still reading, first of all 'Well done'. There are countless ways to be thwarted or hijacked along the way. Corporate attention can wander like that of sleep-deprived toddler. IT departments have a brilliant ability to make everything so slow and expensive that people just give up and KPIs can become so complex that they get ignored. Once your KPI system is up and running it is tempting to think your work is done. It is not. Even successful measurement systems can be derailed and undermined for a wide variety of reasons.

Typical issues with established KPI systems

It can be helpful to look at the things that derail established KPI projects then 'flip' them around to see what we should be doing to avoid those problems.

Here are some of the most serious common issues that kill established management reporting systems:

- **Rapid change of strategy** - KPIs that were once seen as key are no longer regarded as relevant. This happens when measurement systems are not reviewed in parallel with strategy changes.
- **Unexpected disasters or events** - people become distracted by a pressing business emergency and never get back into the routine of gathering and analysing data.
- **Loss of the senior sponsor** - a system kept alive by the will and interest of a senior sponsor rapidly collapses in their absence.
- **'Flat earthers'** - some people just don't believe in management based on data. 'To be honest I believe in gut instinct, rather than measurement' to quote one real-life example I stumbled across.
- **Loss of key specialists** - It may be the 'spreadsheet ninja' that put together a report or a business analyst who had knowledge of SAP. There are certain skills in

most KPI collection systems that are specialist and key to the functioning of the system.

- **Mistrust of output** - As soon as you hear comments like 'That measure is based on dubious data' you should be seriously worried. If unaddressed, lack of trust will very rapidly render reports and dashboards worthless.
- **Entropy** - The non-technical definition of entropy is 'A gradual slide into disorder'. Systems need regular care and attention to work properly. KPI systems, if neglected, will fall into disrepair.

How you can pre-empt your specific issues

I have put together the list above based on my own experience. The process of working out what can go wrong, then flipping it to give us positive actions, is called 'reverse brainstorming'. I find it works because most groups are much more comfortable thinking in practical terms about what goes wrong, rather than what should go right.

Tip

Reverse brainstorming

An approach that works well is to run a 'reverse brainstorming' session with the key stakeholders. Get them to identify the likely issues and remedies. Not only are they likely to come up with a much longer and more comprehensive list, they will automatically be 'bought-in' in a way that they would not if you just lectured them on the issues.

Taking these negatives we can create a set of commitments and behaviours to counter the risk. Taking my examples above:

- **Ensure that every strategy review includes a formal KPI review**. Doing this makes sure that the measures are still guiding the business in the direction we want to go.
- **Set a 'wake up' date for dormant measures and meetings**. It may not be realistic to keep every KPI

running during a complex and traumatic corporate event, such as a merger, but you <u>can</u> commit to a date in the future to review and potentially revive those measures.

- **Spread senior ownership - Make 'flat earth' belief systems culturally unacceptable**. In the same way that it is unacceptable to ignore health and safety principles, it should also become unacceptable to be proud of management by 'gut instinct'. This culture needs to be championed, and demonstrated, by the majority of the senior stakeholders.

- **Identify single-person dependencies in KPI production.** Tools such as the Skills Matrix exist to identify single-person dependencies. Spotting and acting on those risks <u>early</u> helps avoid crisis skills issues.

- **Have a SLA and process for dealing with accuracy issues.** Having a clearly defined process, with agreed service levels, for putting problems right will help sustain confidence in the management information system.

- **Allocate resource to maintenance** - Management systems don't keep running on their own. It is crucial to have an engaged and knowledgeable team member looking after the system after the initial setup. This may not be a full time role, but it is important that they have accountability and are responsible for regular updates on system health and identified issues.

I don't like woolly stuff but....

As you have probably worked out, I don't like woolly metaphysical descriptions, I like tangible specific actions. That's the reason I wrote this book as a series of specific checklists with some fluff in between. Having said that, part of successful KPI implementation is having the **right mindset**. If you have experience with Lean or Six Sigma you will know what I mean. Simply applying tools and checklists will get you some of the way, but after that you need to pay regular, focused, attention to what it is you are trying to achieve. You also need to have a set of principles in the back of your mind. In Lean it is about relentless simplification and reduction of waste.

As a final thought, when it comes to the development of KPIs and reporting systems you can summarise the ideal mindset as:

- Persistent constructive scepticism.
- A bias towards simplicity.
- Desire for structure and order.
- Constant mindfulness of organisational objectives.
- Always remembering that your end customer is a human being.

I hope you found this book useful. Good luck with your future KPI endeavours!

Step 7 - Go live - Sustain

Other useful checklists

Appendix

Appendix

More on meetings

Use meetings for decision-making

Meetings are key engines in all organisations. KPIs and reports are the fuel for those engines. They provide the questions, supporting details and sometimes the explanations. They show whether or not previous meetings have been productive and successful. How you use information in meetings is absolutely central to the improvement cycle.

Meeting behaviour

Particularly where there has been a lack of good quality data in the past, it can take quite a bit of time and effort to change meeting behaviour. Some signs of poor, data-free, meeting behaviour include:

- Frequent shouting.
- The most senior opinion in the room wins.
- Over analysis of problems in the meeting but without evidence or data.
- Failure to agree meaningful and practical actions. Lack of documented actions.
- Regular and serious over-runs of allotted time.
- Senior stakeholders deliberately dodging attending the meeting.

You should have already developed a meeting's Terms of Reference, but if you haven't, refer back to page 67 for the relevant discussion and checklists.

Changing this behaviour will require a sustained and concerted effort. Very often, in good old-fashioned primate style, the room will take all its cues from the most senior person. This is probably the person you need to spend most of your time and effort on.

The Chair plays a key role in keeping the meeting on track.

Rotating Chairs (changing people, not seats that spin round on the spot) are all 'fine and dandy' in theory, but they can really undermine any attempt to change behaviour. You may decide to become a fascist dictatorship, with a static Chair, at least for a few meetings until behaviours have started to change for the better.

Here are some of the things the Chair must do:

Checklist

Chairing meetings

❑ Challenge meeting attendees who are not prepared and have not looked at the data.

❑ Make sure the data is used at the relevant point in each meeting.

❑ Intercept any fruitless arguments with an action to gather the relevant information and data for informed discussion in the next session (if that allows enough time to gather the right information).

❑ Keep the meeting to schedule.

❑ Use techniques such as 'the lightning round' (see below) to stop known 'ramblers' from dominating the meeting with long and pointless monologues.

If meetings regularly run over you need to consider whether they are all badly run or whether the time slot is long enough to discuss everything that needs to be covered.

Do the reports make sense?

I have often been in the situation where reports are impenetrable and difficult to read. I used to think it was just me being stupid but discovered, through experience, that the 'insiders' in an organisation often feel the same, but are afraid to admit it. Here's a quick way of analysing the situation using five questions.

Checklist

Are your reports understandable?

❏ Does the report makes sense to you?

❏ Have you asked the internal customers whether the report makes sense to them?

❏ Has the report or dashboard been tested on an intelligent but non-specialist layperson?

❏ Have you specifically asked the internal customers how the clarity of the report could be improved?

❏ Does the report or dashboard require specialist briefing? If so, how does someone who has not had that briefing access it easily?

Trap

Keep stakeholders 'on-side'

No-one likes to be cornered, especially in front of their boss. Think very carefully about how information can be shared in a way that gives everyone the opportunity to 'do the right thing' and prepare properly for the meeting rather than being broadsided by unexpected and unwelcome results.

Tip

The meeting lightning round

This is a technique used in meetings when individuals required to give an update are prone to rambling on for far too long. Very simply, you give a fixed interval to each of the contributors in which they must give their update. Typically this will be 60 seconds. Doesn't sound like much time but, with prior thought and preparation, it's surprising how much useful information can be packed into a short period. The key phrases here are **prior thought** and **preparation**. These behaviours are exactly what the lightning round is intended to promote. It should help avoid 'winging it' and highlight when people are doing so.

Assess meeting relevancy

Two of the most common criticisms of meetings are that they are long and tedious. The root cause of this may well be that the meeting scope is poorly defined and that many of the points in the meeting are not relevant to most of the people in that meeting.

If you have a suspicion that your meeting may be too broad and too long, I suggest that you create a relevancy matrix. This consists of the attendees on one axis and the main topics of discussion on the other. You then add a status icon (smileys in the example below) next to each name and topic, where the topic is relevant to that individual. Here's a very simple version, to give you a flavour:

Topic	CEO	Head of Risk	Head of IT	Head of NPD	Head of Finance	Head of Sales	Head of Legal
Financial performance	Relevant	Some Relevance	Some Relevance	Some Relevance	Relevant	Relevant	Not relevant
Complaints	Relevant	Relevant	Some Relevance	Not relevant	Not relevant	Relevant	Relevant
Health and safety	Relevant	Relevant	Not relevant	Some Relevance	Not relevant	Not relevant	Relevant
Legal	Relevant	Relevant	Not relevant	Relevant	Not relevant	Not relevant	Relevant

(Attendee)

Fig. 8.1: A meeting relevancy matrix

If you decide to fix a relevancy problem, you have a couple of options:

- Section the meeting, so that certain people are brought in for certain relevant sections but not all of it.
- Spin off various elements of the current meeting into separate meetings.

You can download a free meeting relevancy matrix template from here: **http://wp.me/p1H6XP-zD**

Debate in meetings

Debate is good but too much debate is deadly. There is a fine line to be trodden between good healthy discussion and paralysing indecision. Unfortunately there is no clear-cut rule here; it comes down to the skill of the Chair. This is another reason to find a good Chair and stick with them rather than rotating on a meeting-by-meeting basis.

Do all the meeting participants really understand what is being discussed?

This is a topic I rarely hear being discussed but is a real issue in many organisations. At some point in the organisational hierarchy it becomes unacceptable to admit that you do not understand something. There are sometimes legitimate reasons for not understanding what is presented - for instance, it may be complete and utter cobblers. Unfortunately, hierarchical deference means that unintelligible or incomprehensible data can be presented and accepted without meaningful challenge, in the style of the 'emperor's new clothes'.

Meeting rules

I'm no meeting fascist. I realise that meetings are not just about decision-making, they are also social (sharp intake of breath). Rules can help keep things on track, especially if they are formulated and agreed by the participants. Here are some typical rules that you may, or may not, want to stick to.

Checklist

Example meeting rules checklist

❏ Agenda and data issued x days (hours) before the meeting.

❏ Expectation of 'arrive on time or don't come'.

❏ Listen to every contribution.

❏ One person speaks at a time.

❏ Phones and computers off.

❏ Take problem solving outside the meeting.

❏ Actions and minutes issued within two hours of meeting end.

❏ Review previous actions.

It's worth reiterating that most meeting behaviour isn't determined by the written rules but by the competence and behaviour of the Chair - so choose that person very carefully.

Ad hoc reporting requests

One of the big challenges I have seen repeatedly is a steady stream of ad hoc requests that come into Management Information/KPI teams that I have worked with. The requests are usually to support meetings, driven by pressing business needs and requested by very senior people, so just saying 'no' isn't on the cards.

Here are some steps that can help put some structure to the discussion if these requests are seriously impairing departmental 'business as usual'.

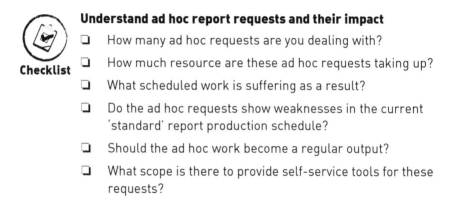

Checklist

Understand ad hoc report requests and their impact

❏ How many ad hoc requests are you dealing with?

❏ How much resource are these ad hoc requests taking up?

❏ What scheduled work is suffering as a result?

❏ Do the ad hoc requests show weaknesses in the current 'standard' report production schedule?

❏ Should the ad hoc work become a regular output?

❏ What scope is there to provide self-service tools for these requests?

Capture meeting actions

This is not strictly KPI-related, but it is important. Managing actions effectively is absolutely crucial. If your meeting does not generate well-defined actions then you should question whether it is adding any value.

Checklist

Meeting actions checklist

❏ Is there an agreed person/method for recording actions?

❏ Is the action description clearly captured?

❏ Is the reason for the action captured?

❏ Is the action assigned to a specific person?

❏ Is there a timescale assigned to the action?

❏ Are previous actions formally reviewed and updated?

Appendix - More on meetings

Bibliography

Books

Much of the presentation style I use, both in this book and in the dashboards and reports I design, has been strongly influenced by the following books:

How to Make an IMPACT: Influence, Inform and Impress with Your Reports, Presentations and Business Documents

Financial Times Series
Author   Jon Moon
Publisher   Financial Times/ Prentice Hall
ISBN 0273713329, 9780273713326

Jon Moon's book is a highly readable and practical book on how to present text, tables and diagrams. An absolute must if you want to free yourself from the tyranny of bullet points and template-sameness.

Information Dashboard Design: The Effective Visual Communication of Data

O'Reilly Series
Safari Books Online
Author   Stephen Few
Publisher   O'Reilly Media Incorporated
ISBN   0596100167, 9780596100162

Many of the ideas I use in my 'BlinkReporting' approach come from Stephen Few's book. It's more of a source book than a bedtime read, but it is a very useful source of ideas and examples.

The Visual Display of Quantitative Information

Author   Edward R. Tufte
Publisher   Graphics Press USA
ISBN   0961392142, 9780961392147

This is a classic from the father of Sparklines. If I'm honest, it's the book I read least as it has a fairly dense academic feel to it. However, you cannot fault Tufte's ideas or influence. Worth owning just for the fabulous quality of the physical book!

The Checklist Manifesto: How to Get Things Right

Author   Atul Gawande
Publisher   Profile Books
ISBN   1846683149, 9781846683145

This is probably the most 'un-put-downable' of the books on this list. It is a very compelling argument in favour of using checklists in most complex professional environments (yes, MI department, I'm looking at you!)

HBR's 10 Must Reads On Strategy

Author   Harvard Business Review
Publisher   Harvard Business School Press
ISBN   9781422157985, 1422157989

This is a clear, simple and really well-written set of articles on the fundamentals of strategy. A classic (and readable) text.

P-M Analysis

Authors   Kunio Shirose, Mitsugu Kaneda, Yoshifumi Kimura
Publisher   Productivity Press, 2004
ISBN   1563273128, 9781563273124

P-M analysis is a very obscure TPM (Total Productive Maintenance) methodology for solving very complex problems. It deserves to be much better known as it is peerless for very tough process-based problems. I've used it for nearly 20 years and find it onerous but indispensable in the right situation.

Articles

When the Fortress Went Down
By Phillip S. Meilinger
http://www.airforcemag.com/MagazineArchive/Pages/2004/
October%202004/1004fortress.aspx

Atul Gawande talked about the history of checklists in 'The Checklist Manifesto'. I went back to this web article he referenced and used many of the details from it to write my introduction for this book.

Index

Lightning Source UK Ltd.
Milton Keynes UK
UKHW030656021121
393250UK00015B/921

9 781910 047002